CITY 'TIL I DIE

BY DAVID CHIDLOW

IT WAS THE

GREATEST MOMENT

IT WAS THE GREATEST MOMENT because of the very manner of the victory. Roy of the Rovers never featured in such a finale. Things like that only happen against us. We are the experts at snatching humiliation from the jaws of a comfortable victory. We are the masters of forcing journalists to rewrite the whole report in the light of a last minute collapse. When it comes to throwing it away, we throw it further and more often than anyone else. But just for once, when it really mattered, we revived the corpse of our season, just as the out-of-body experience was turning into a vision of hell. Just for once, we conjured ecstasy from the devastation, we contrived a win just when defeat was leering at us in mockery.

IT WAS THE GREATEST MOMENT because it was pure, unadulterated City, a substance too potent even for hardened addicts. We'd gone through the full emotional gamut and come out the other end raw and stripped of all reserve. Tears flowed in abundance, great big clown's tears, down faces red with beer and emotion.

IT WAS THE GREATEST MOMENT because it was the most important in the club's history. Because we won, we can now look back upon our flirtation with the lower reaches of English football as nothing more than a temporary aberration, a lapse, an endearing peccadillo. We have flirted with the lower depths and have now left them behind forever. But what if we had to endure yet another season in football's 'nether-nether' land? What effect would it have had on the club's financial situation? How would it have limited the range of players prepared to join the club? How many potential investors would still have considered us a viable investment? How long would it have been before the likes of Nicky Weaver and Gerard Wiekens were sold to balance the books?

IT WAS THE GREATEST MOMENT because the victory was all the sweeter after tasting the bitterness of defeat in those last nine minutes. I'll never forget that moment when Weaver saved the final penalty. It's indelibly imprinted on my mind by the stamp of pure joy. I looked up to the sky and knew that God was in heaven, that justice and goodness reign and that I am one of the blessed, one of the favoured. A benign force was smiling down on us, and in that moment all wrongs were righted, all disappointments wiped away. It's the best day City have ever given me.

Joe O'Neill

BLUES EVERYWHERE.

EVERY PERSON. EVERY CAR. EVERY BUS.

MANCHESTER WAS ON THE MOVE.

IT WAS THE CITY OF MANCHESTER'S DAY.

MAKE NO MISTAKE, THIS WAS MANCHESTER'S DAY.

GORDON STUART-COLE.

THE ONLY
FOOTBALL TEAM
CITY
TO COME FROM
MANCHESTER

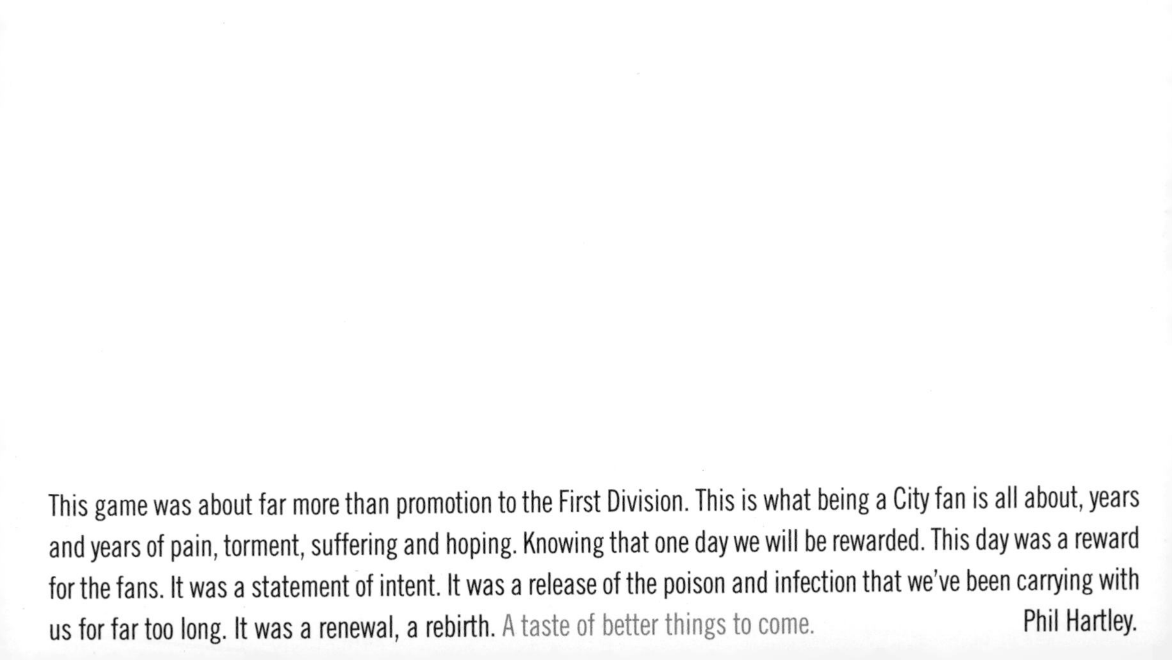

This game was about far more than promotion to the First Division. This is what being a City fan is all about, years and years of pain, torment, suffering and hoping. Knowing that one day we will be rewarded. This day was a reward for the fans. It was a statement of intent. It was a release of the poison and infection that we've been carrying with us for far too long. It was a renewal, a rebirth. A taste of better things to come.

Phil Hartley.

BALL CLUB
1883
ORS TERRACE
RS V MANCHESTER CITY
BALL LEAGUE DIVISION TWO
No. 00651
SATURDAY 1ST MAY 1999
3:00 PM K.O.
You are advised to take up your
an hour before the kick-off.
PRESTON NORTH END P.L.C.
PNE V MANCHESTER CITY
NATIONWIDE LEAGUE DIVISION TWO
MON 05 APR 1999 KICK OFF 12:00 P.M.
BILL SHANKLY KOP BLOCK K
ROW
20
SEAT
7
PRICE
£13.00
PR0123866
VISITORS
ENTER THROUGH
ACCLESFIELD TOWN
V
MANCHESTER CITY
OSS ROSE GROUND, MACCLESFIELD
ATURDAY 12th SEPTEMBER 1998
Kick-Off 3.00pm
Nationwide
2
ADULT £10.00 JUNIOR/SEN.CIT. £6.0
SILKMAN TERRACE
0022
adejski Stadium
ng v Manchester
City
7 Mar 99 **KICKOFF 1:00PM**
(Red) BLOCK : R28
ED SEATING
83 £12.00
AFC Bournemouth
NATIONWIDE LEAGUE DIV 2
SEWARD
ROVER - MG
Club Shirt Sponsors
AFCB V MANCHESTER CITY
13 Feb, 1999
kick off: 3:00
MATCH SPONSOR: HEATHLAN
Brighton Beach
Nationwide
row seat:
please retain fo
DEAN COURT GROUND BOURNE

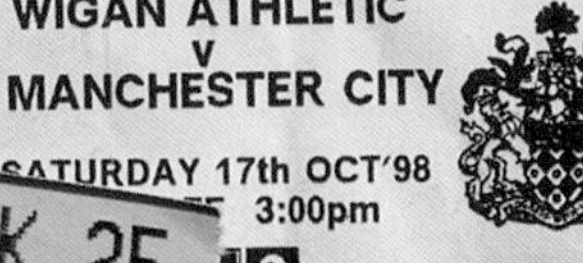
PHOENIX STAND
(AWAY)
WIGAN ATHLETIC
V
MANCHESTER CITY
SATURDAY 17th OCT'98
3:00pm
2
CONC.
£ 6.00
TICKET No.
00018
ATHLETIC AFC LTD.
OLDHAM
Mr J.T. Cal
WHERE APPROP
PLEASE TAKE UP YOU
LATICS CLUBCALL
0891 121142
NATIONWIDE
TER CITY F.C.
TESTIMONIAL
ERLAND
KICK OFF 03:00 P.M.
PRICE
£10.00
010798 WW
NORTH UPPER BLOCK 25
TURNSTILES
D31-36
£ 11.00
£ 11.00
ADULT ROW SEAT
NATIONWIDE LEAGUE DIV TWO
MILLWALL
V MANCHESTER CITY
KICK OFF

Bootham Crescent, York.
VAT No. 170 1075 04
MAIN STAND
SECTION C
ROW G
SEAT 10
YORK CITY FC
Stoke City Football Club
Britannia Stadium
NATIONWIDE LEAGUE DIVISION TWO
VERSUS MANCHESTER CITY
FRI 29 JAN 1999 KICK OFF 07:45 P.M.
SIGNAL RADIO STAND BLOCK 37
ROW SEAT PRICE
30 898 £14.00
KOP STAN
SOLD SUBJECT TO
SECURITY
AWAY SUPPORTERS ONLY TERRACE
ENTRANCE VIA : REDFERN AVENUE
GILLINGHAM F.C.
V MANCHESTER CITY
KICK-OFF 3:00 p.m.
ADULT £9.50
OAP/JUV £7.50 / 4.50
TICKET NUMBER 00203
Nationwide 2
LUTON TOWN FOOTBALL CLUB
TO BE RETAINED
WALSALL FC
NATIONWIDE LEAGUE
Walsall versus Man
SAT 23 JAN 1999
WILLIAM SHARP STAN
AREA ROW SEAT
W9 D 048
ENTER BY TURNSTILE
Oldham Athletic A.F.C. Ltd.
Oldham OL1 2PA
STAND
LATICS TICKET NEWS 0891 121582
TURNSTILE 23/28
BLOCK SEATS
ROW A
SEAT 000018
PRICE
DIVISION TWO
NOVEMBER 1998
DARLINGTON F.C.
FEETHAMS, DARLINGTON, DL1 5JB.
DARLINGTON V MANCHESTER CITY
F.A. CUP ROUND TWO Sponsored By AXA
FRIDAY 4TH DECEMBER 1998 K.O.8:00 PM
ADMIT TO WEST STAND SEATS
TICKET NO:83
ADULT £ 11.00
CONCESSION £ 6.00
COLCHESTER UNITED
Layer Road, Colchester, CO2 7JJ
Colchester United F.C.
vs MANCHESTER CITY
Sat 20 MAR 1999
BLOCK E
ROW C

FULHAM V MANCHESTER CITY
FRI 14 AUG 1998 Kick Off 07:45 P.M
PUTNEY TERRACE
STANDING
£10.00
TO BE RETAINED
Main Club Sponsor: EDS
WORTHINGTON CUP 2nd ROUND 1st LEG
DERBY COUNTY V MANCHESTER CITY
Wednesday, 16th September, 1998 Kick-off 7.45 pm
MANSFIELD BITTER UPPER
PRICE 19.00
ENTER VIA TURNSTILE 51 TO 54
STAIR 58
ROW N
SEAT 0697
Meadow Lane, Nottingham
SEAT 7
1998
BLACKPOOL FOOTBALL CLUB
Club Sponsors TELEWEST
BLACKPOOL VS MANCHESTER CITY
NATIONWIDE LEAGUE DIVISION TWO
SAT 09 JAN 1999 KICK OFF 12:00
EAST PADDOCK SOUTH
REF:EPS41006
PRICE
STANDING ONLY £10.00
TURNSTILES: ENTER VIA ENTRANCE 7
NORTHAMPTON TOWN
NATIONWIDE LEAGUE
Sat, 26/09/1998
SOUTH STAND TURNSTILE
CLUB CALL
CHARGED AT 50P
SHEVINGTON END TERRACE
TURNSTILES 10A,10B,11A,11B
VISITORS SECTION (Uncovered)
WIGAN ATHLETIC
v
MANCHESTER CITY
SATURDAY 15th MAY.99
DIVISION TWO PLAY-OFF
FIRST LEG
Nationwide 2
ADULT £ 7.50
U16/OAP £ 4.00
TICKET No. 003
WIGAN ATHLETIC AFC LTD.
SPRINGFIELD PARK, WIGAN, WN6 7BA
UNRESERVED
Cer City
KICK OFF
ITED F.C.
all League
R CITY
6.00 p.m
GUARDIAN DIRECT/ ASHBY'S
BLOCK E
WREXHAM A.F.C. LIMITED
NATIONWIDE FOOTBALL LEAGUE
MANCHESTER CITY
SAT 26 DEC 1998 KICK-OFF 12:00 PM
MARSTON STAND
TURNSTILES 41 & 42
ROW P
SEAT 104
PRICE £12.00
Nationwide
RECREATION GROUND
CROSS ST. TERRACE
CHESTERFIELD F.C.
v
MANCHESTER CITY F.C.
SATURDAY 27th FEBRUARY 1999
KICK-OFF 3:00pm
VISITORS
KENNING

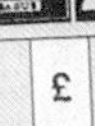

At the top of Wembley Way I turned and looked around, back towards the tube station. I stood there, frozen to the spot, for about 5 minutes with a ridiculous grin on my face. This was what we'd been waiting for. This was the reason we'd been to all those games at all those awful grounds this year. This was why we hadn't slunk off and supported someone else after the second relegation in three seasons. It was my chance to see City at Wembley, to stand at the top of Wembley Way and watch the expectant crowd make their way towards the ground, to finally realise my dream that I could one day see City play again where the heroes of the past had done so well.

Sharon Hargreaves.

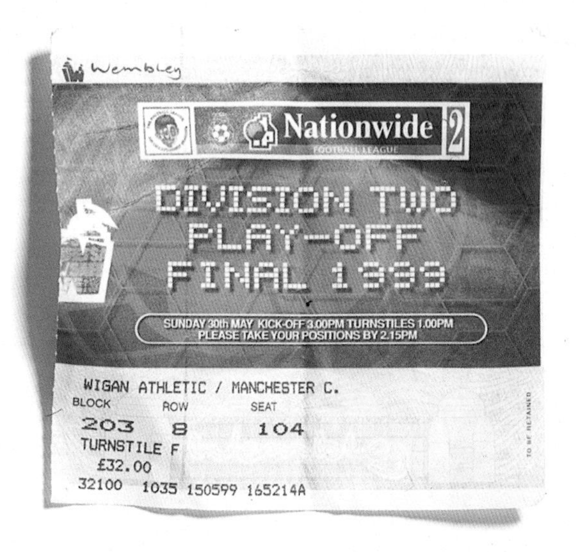

DIVISION 2 PLAY-OFF

The teams coming out. The procession of players, looking so small and vulnerable in the middle of all the razzmatazz of Fatboy Slim, fireworks, balloons, and the unbelievable crowd delirium....

...and then the way it became just another football match as soon as the whistle blew. The heartfelt singing turning into the usual grumblings about Edghill, Whitley, Goater et al.

Pat Poynton

What's your abiding memory of that May afternoon?

Over the years when I have been to Wembley for Cup Finals etc. I have looked at the reds, whites and blacks of the supporters at either end of the ground and dreamt of their being replaced by our Blue. It was fantastic supporters having a great day and feeling that our Club was taking a first step back into the big time.

When you saw the Blue Army enmasse at Wembley, how did you feel? What contribution do you believe they made to the result?

I had dreamt all season about our playing at Wembley. This had always been my preferred route to promotion as I felt it would be a great boost for the Club. I feel our fans were instrumental in our winning both at Wembley and against Wigan. We were fortunate that the penalties were at our end. Shooting into that goal must have been an intimidating experience.

At 0-2, facing 'certain' defeat what were you thinking/feeling/doing?

Glancing at the giant Wembley scoreboard and trying to blank out the singing from the Gillingham fans. My mind was racing with thoughts about next season and the need to hold things together.

What does the battle cry 'City 'til I die' mean to you?

In sporting terms City are the only thing that matters to me. In 1966 I upset most of my friends by telling them that City's next match meant more to me than England winning the World Cup. Certainly my devotion to City will last as long as I do.

David Bernstein.

(THE FIRST HALF ISN'T WORTH MENTIONING)

GRAHAM.

Having spent over £250 listening to the Wigan games over the telephone, I decided to sod the expense and journey from South Africa to watch my team. I phoned my Dad, who lives in Huddersfield, is sixty-five, disabled and has been a City fan all his days. I told him to meet me at King's Cross. We were going to Wembley, a place he had never been, to watch his beloved City.

This is not a story about my journey , but about my Dad.

We lived for over twenty-six years at 61 Thornton Road, literally spitting distance from the Football Academy and would still be there today, but for the untimely death of my Mother late in 1988. Since then, I have moved abroad, Dad got re-married and we spend precious little time together, however the little time we do is normally spent talking about City. With the distance between us, coupled with the poor performance of City , it would be fair to say that our relationship has been less than buoyant for many a long year.

So, Saturday night at six, my mate Allan and I set off from Johannesburg to worship the Blues. We started quite brilliantly with an upgrade on the 'plane and in true Manc fashion I declined the Champagne in favour of Lager. About three hours later we were asked rather politely to sit down and stop chanting, "Who the **** are Man United?" After two public warnings we succumbed, took the sleeping pills and awoke six hours later on landing at Heathrow. After the journey through London to meet Dad, Allan asked me if I was going to tell everyone in London why we were here (a reference to my informing all I met that we were going to watch the only football team to come from Manchester). As Dad ambled down the platform, off the Leeds train , with a huge smile and his sports bag full of sandwiches and Yorkies, I felt like his son again. We travelled to Wembley , via The Green Man for two hours of swally, on the tube with lots of Blues, Dad even met a lad whose father used to play for City, which allowed him to impress all present with his deep knowledge and love of the club.

On arrival at Wembley we sauntered up the Way with so many, many fans, it was incredible. My mates from Moss Side brought the tickets as promised, time for some fish and chips and then onto the game. What happened over the next two hours has already gone down in football history as astonishing. Rather than repeat other well chosen words let me say this. I smiled from start to finish, proud to be with my Dad, proud of my club, and most proud of its unique supporters. I turned to Dad in the 88th minute and said something along the lines of, "What a great day out for us, it cannot end like this." He in turn looked at me tearfully and said, "Yes, a great day son, but that is City for you." Over the next eight minutes, we seemed to just stand with arms aloft or around each other or some similar soul. As the penalties came, we helped Dad up to stand on the bench, held him tight and I whispered, " now see a bit of history." He looked and laughed, me the eternal optimist, him the reverse. Ten minutes later we were all crying with joy. I couldn't help feeling that this was what we all deserved after the awful disappointment of the last decades. As we moved back to King's Cross, we sang and danced and chanted with our fellow Blues, so much that we never wanted the journey to end.

We arrived at King's Cross with ten minutes to spare, Dad got on the train and I ran along the platform with a bottle of gin in my hand waving goodbye and mouthing "I love you." He just waved back, smiling and shaking his head as he explained to the people opposite that this was his mad City fan son from South Africa, I simply cried. My mate Allan was also crying as I walked back up towards the station and I asked him why, "You just looked like a ten year-old again." he replied. Ironic, but that was exactly how I felt, like the days when we would leave the ground and walk down the pink passage together after City had won. My Dad was the best in the world and me and him were City fans. I know that still to be true, thanks for everything Dad.

Mark Bell

I remember thinking "...only nine minutes left. whoever scores first will win..."

only to see Asaba running up the field and slotting home. Jagdeep Gil

SHARP
SHARP
MANCHESTER
UNITED
SHARP
SHARP
SHARP

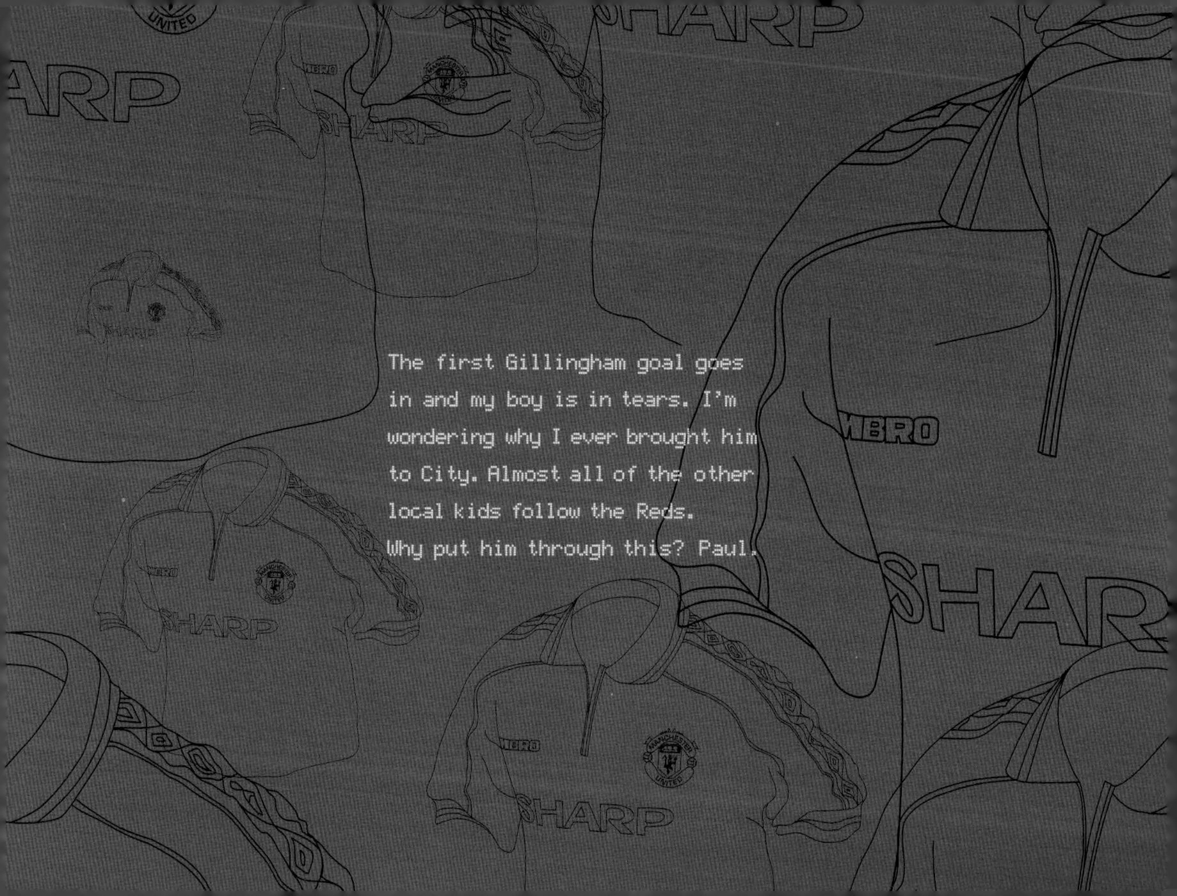

The first Gillingham goal goes in and my boy is in tears. I'm wondering why I ever brought him to City. Almost all of the other local kids follow the Reds. Why put him through this? Paul.

I had seen Scunthorpe win the previous day, and was thinking to myself. It looks like we're playing 'Scunny' next season.

Joe Royle

'Barry'

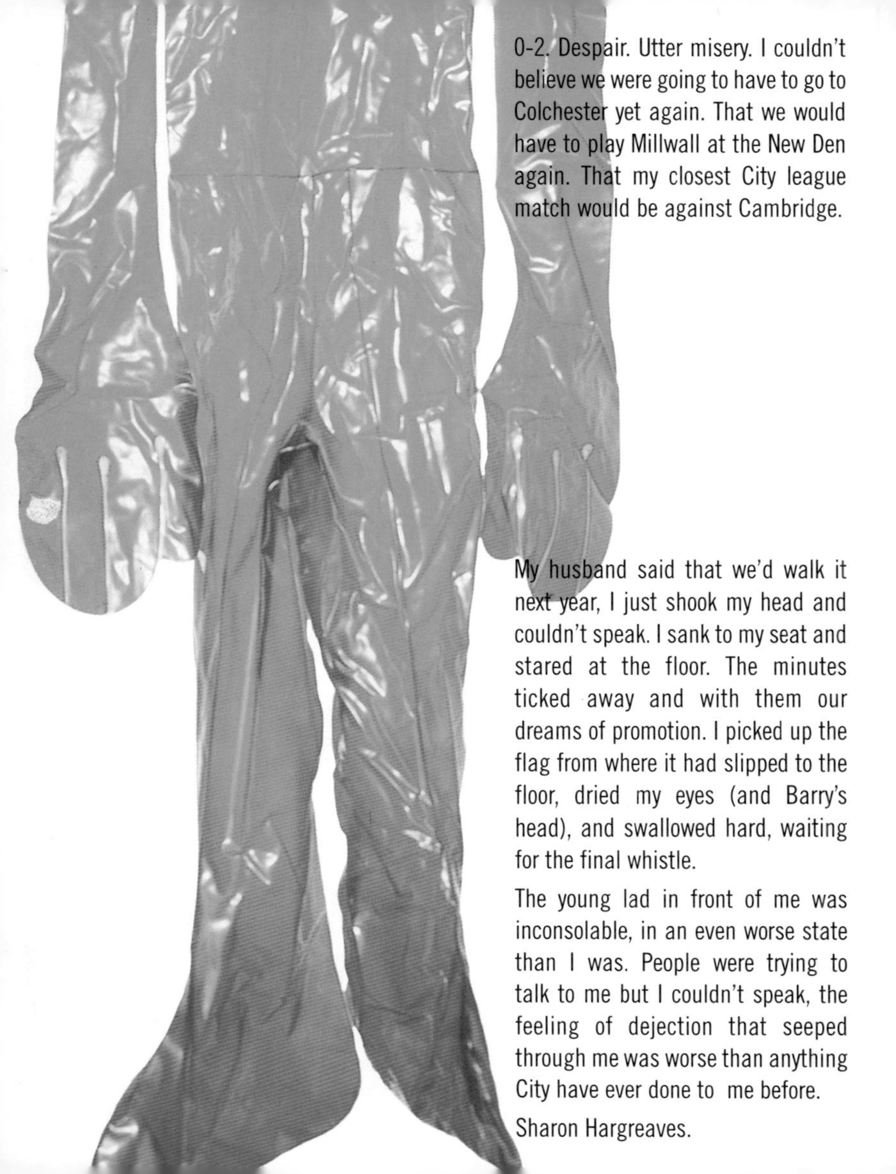

0-2. Despair. Utter misery. I couldn't believe we were going to have to go to Colchester yet again. That we would have to play Millwall at the New Den again. That my closest City league match would be against Cambridge.

My husband said that we'd walk it next year, I just shook my head and couldn't speak. I sank to my seat and stared at the floor. The minutes ticked away and with them our dreams of promotion. I picked up the flag from where it had slipped to the floor, dried my eyes (and Barry's head), and swallowed hard, waiting for the final whistle.

The young lad in front of me was inconsolable, in an even worse state than I was. People were trying to talk to me but I couldn't speak, the feeling of dejection that seeped through me was worse than anything City have ever done to me before.

Sharon Hargreaves.

At 0-2, facing 'certain' defeat, what did you do?

I WENT TO THE KITCHEN AND MADE A POT OF TEA

Joyce Johnstone

2-0. Down I wanted to go home
I could'nt stand watching any more.
A huge feeling of dissapointment for
everybody

Janet Kirby

Born in

I was too young to be a part of 1976 and so far have only experienced torment and pain. 20 long years of expectation. Another 20 years of being laughed at, but still always holding my head up, knowing it would come right.

It all rested on this day.

Sunday was going to be the day I could start feeling positive again. The day I could turn their laughter back at them. But now it had all been cruelly ripped away from me.

A bloke behind me screamed, "You've let us down again, you've let us down big time".

Elaine Clegg

OUR KID GIVES IT TO ME AFTER HORLOCK'S GOAL, "BOLLOX, THAT JUST SUGAR COATS IT. I'D RATHER GET BEATEN 2-0 THAN 2-1". FLORIDA BLUE.

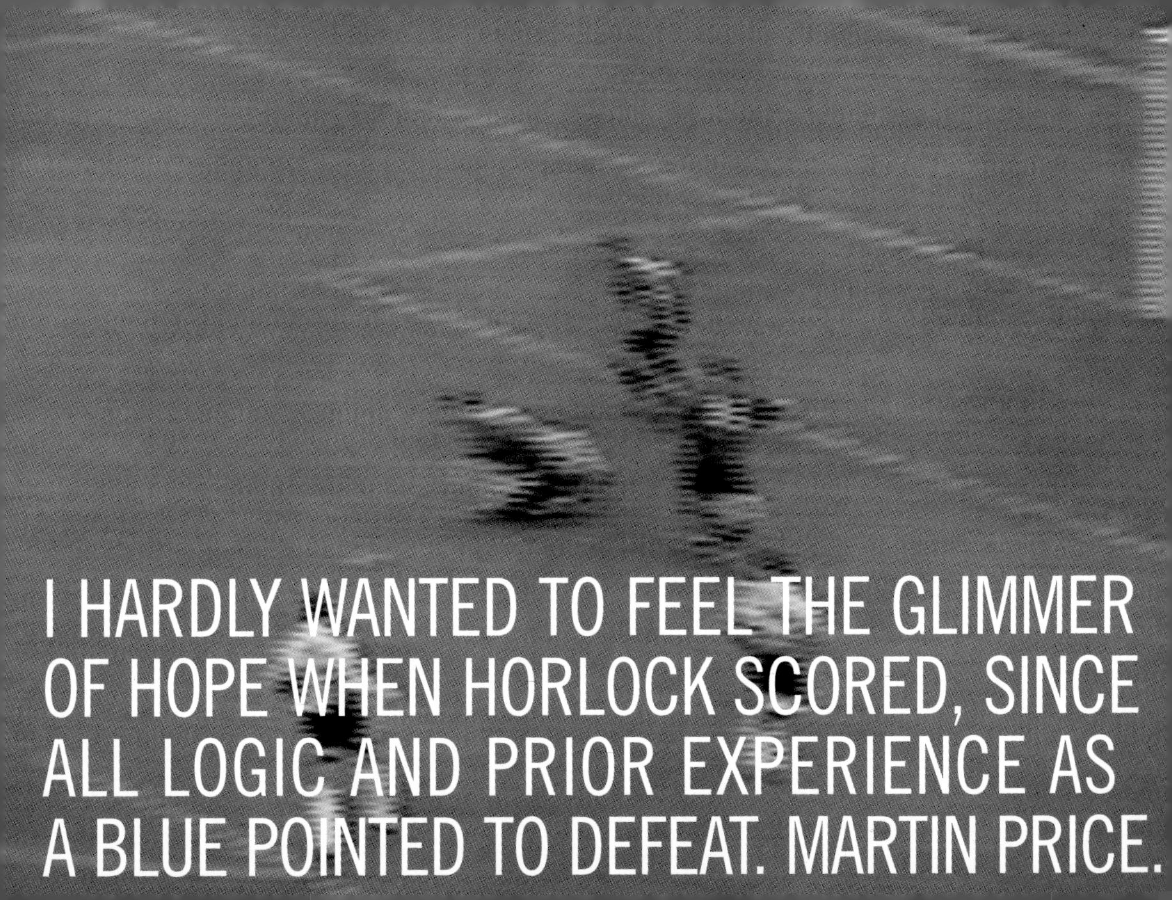
I HARDLY WANTED TO FEEL THE GLIMMER
OF HOPE WHEN HORLOCK SCORED, SINCE
ALL LOGIC AND PRIOR EXPERIENCE AS
A BLUE POINTED TO DEFEAT. MARTIN PRICE.

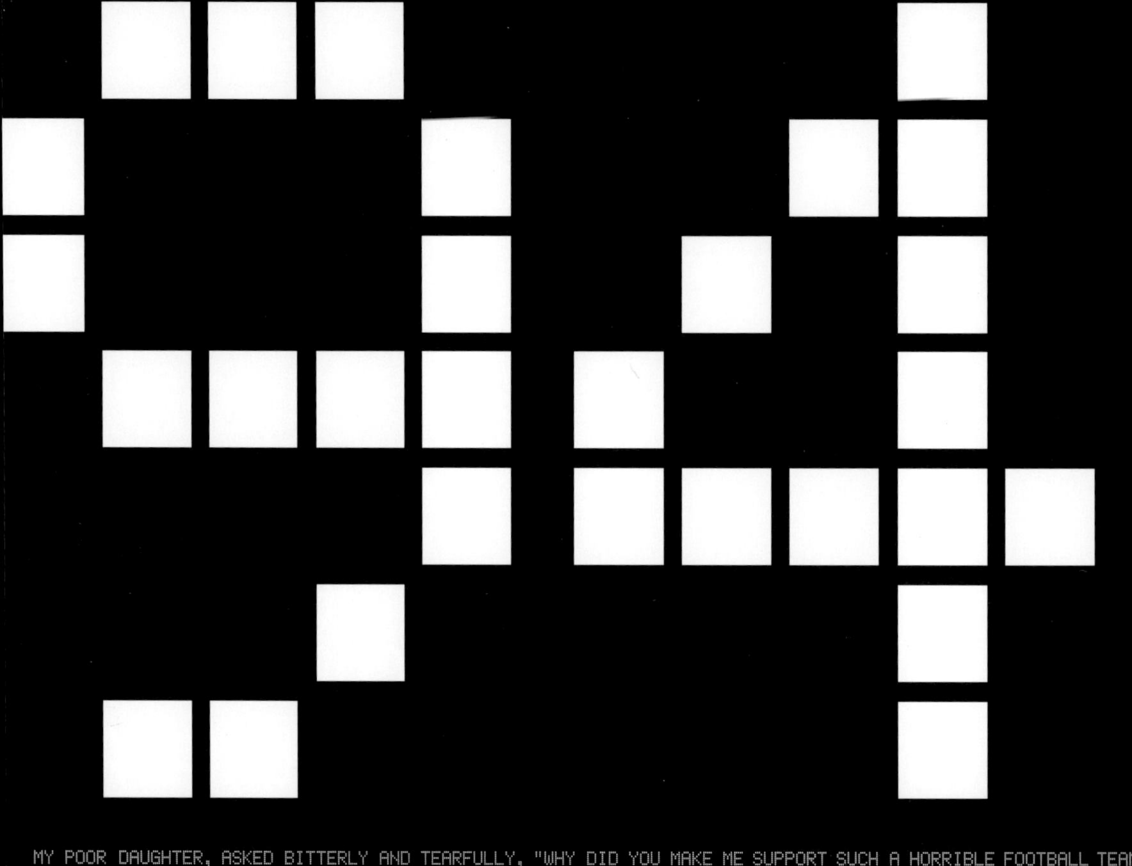
MY POOR DAUGHTER, ASKED BITTERLY AND TEARFULLY, "WHY DID YOU MAKE ME SUPPORT SUCH A HORRIBLE FOOTBALL TEA

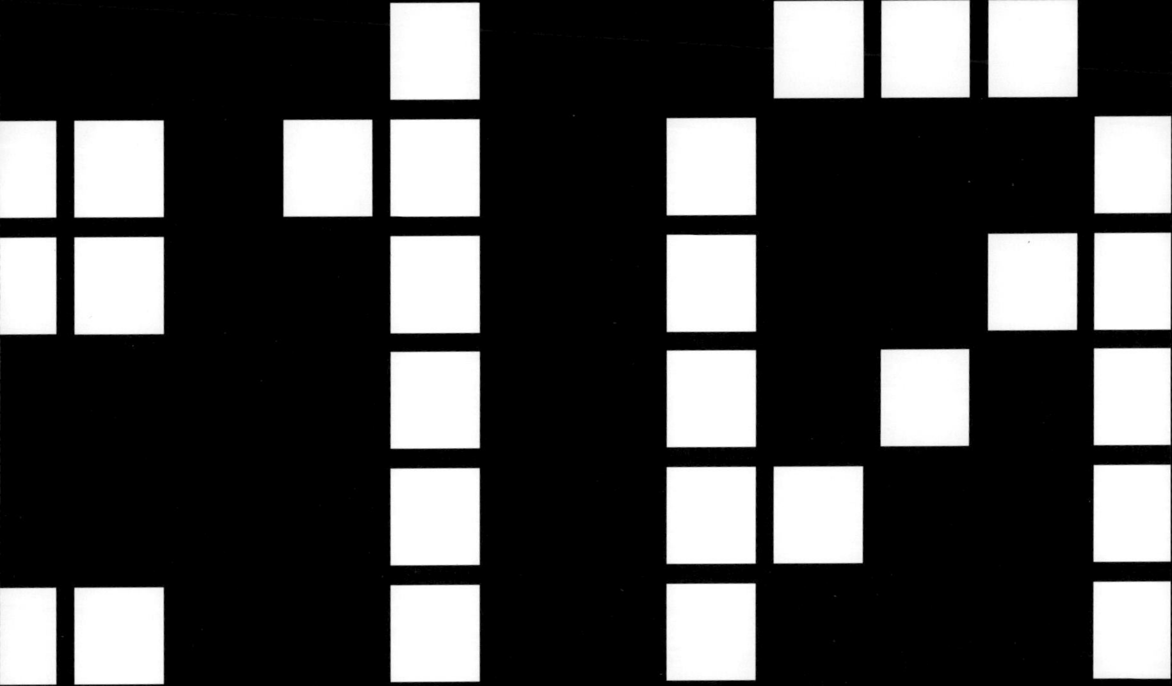

THEN TIME STOOD STILL. EVERYONE, INCLUDING ME, WAS SCREAMING FOR DICKOV TO SHOOT, BUT THERE WAS NO SOUND. IT WAS LIKE ONE OF THOSE DREAM SEQUENCES IN A FILM; SOFT FOCUS, SLOW MOTION AND DISTANT, INDISTINCT ECHOES OF SOUND.

PHIL HARTLEY.

"THE WHITE MITRE BALL STREAKED ACROSS THE WEMBLEY TURF CARRYING ALL THE HOPES AND FRUSTRATIONS OF THE BETTER HALF OF THE BEST CITY IN THE WORLD..." SIMON QUAYLE
OH, N
GILLS
GILLINGH
Kool
Kool
brother
brother

OOOOO!
Mitre
CITY
MC
FC
men in blue
brother
Kool
KIPPAX
eidos

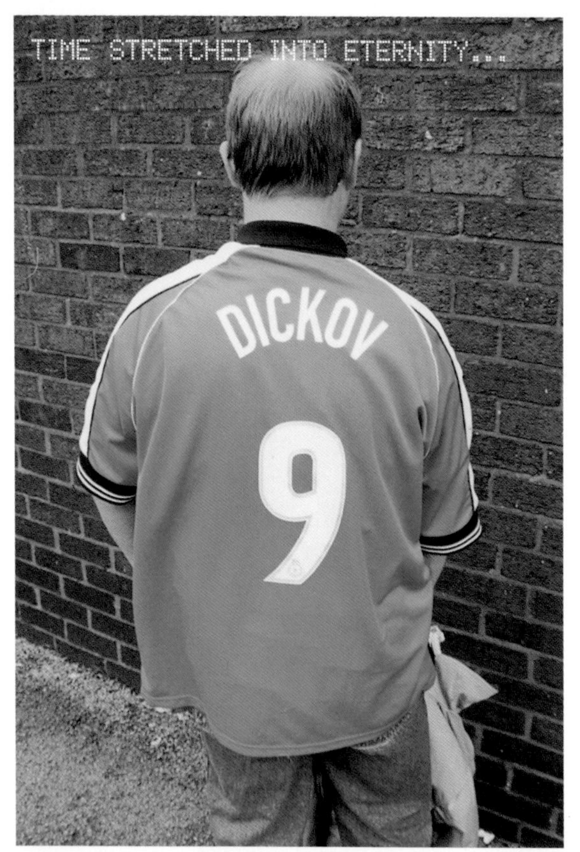
TIME STRETCHED INTO ETERNITY...
DICKOV
9

DICKOV
9
UNTIL THAT MAGIC MOMENT

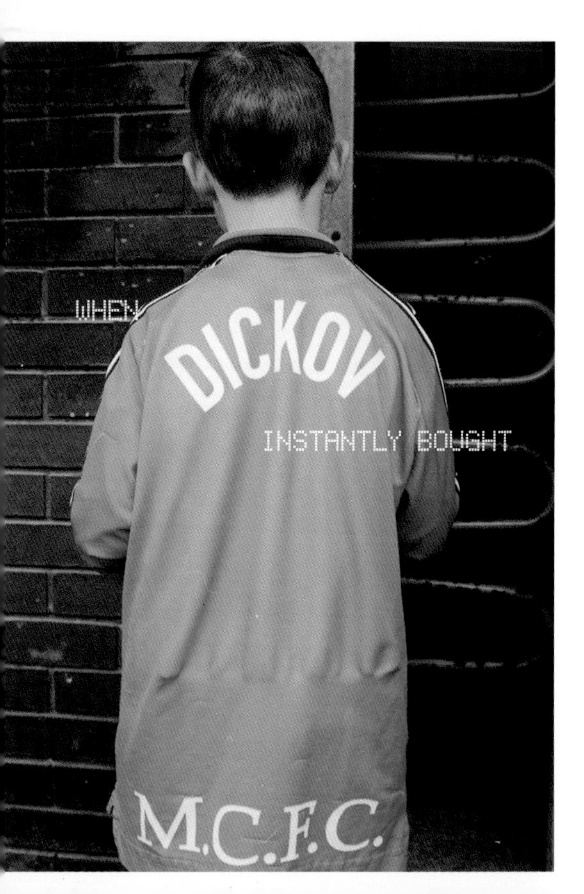

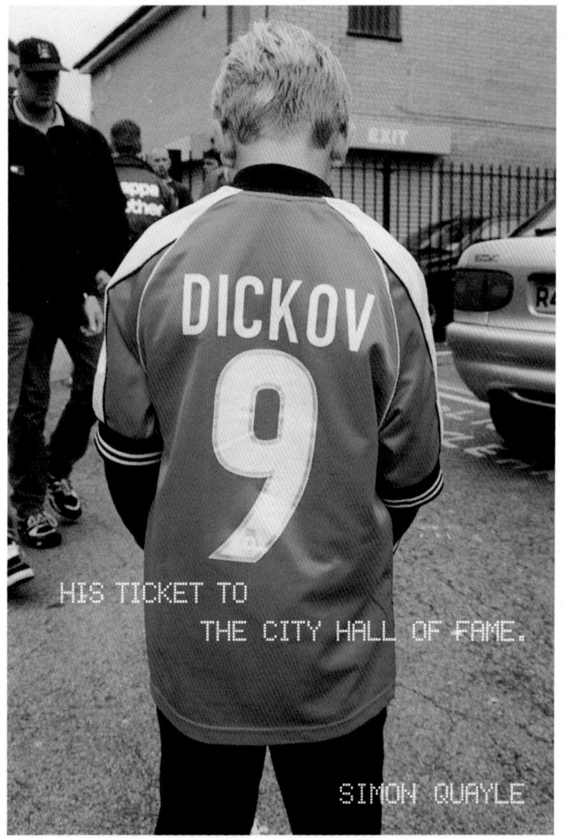

WHEN

INSTANTLY BOUGHT

HIS TICKET TO

THE CITY HALL OF FAME.

SIMON QUAYLE

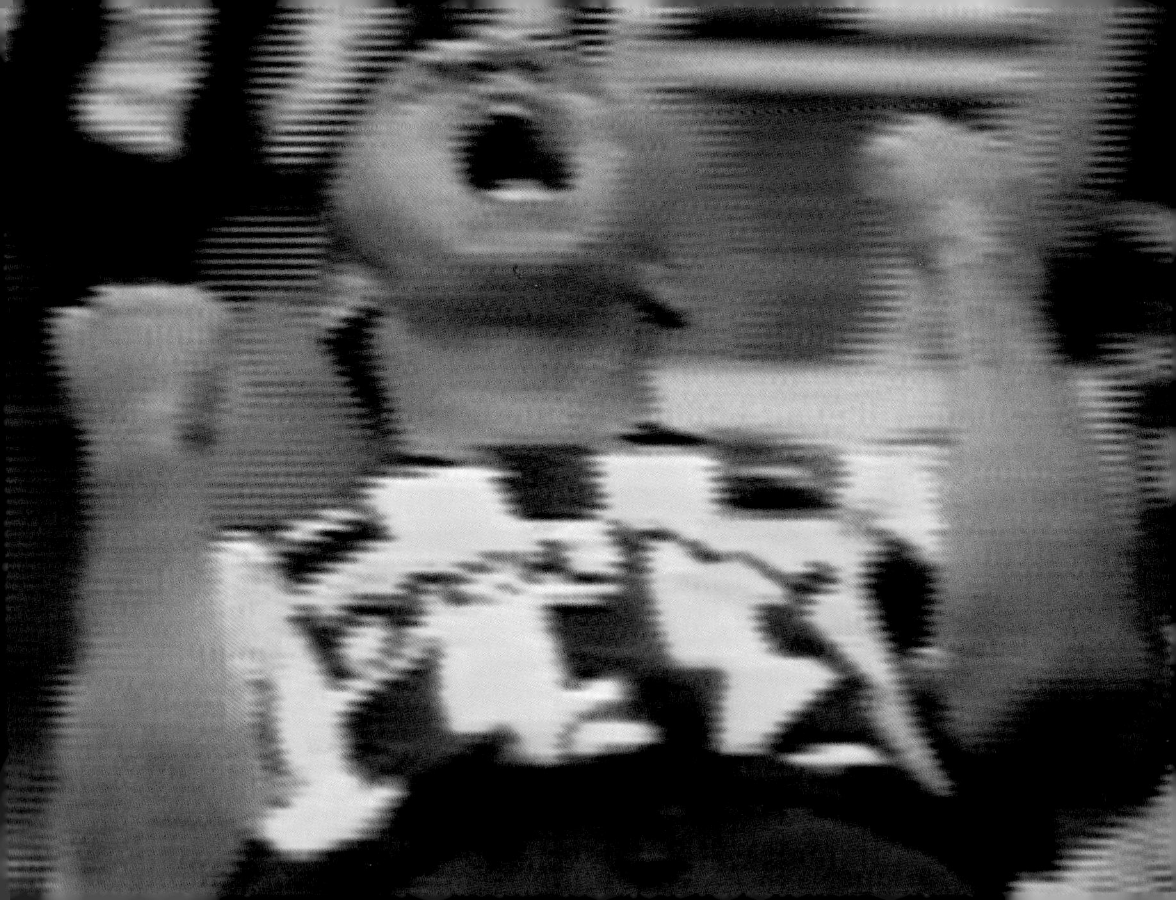

IUM

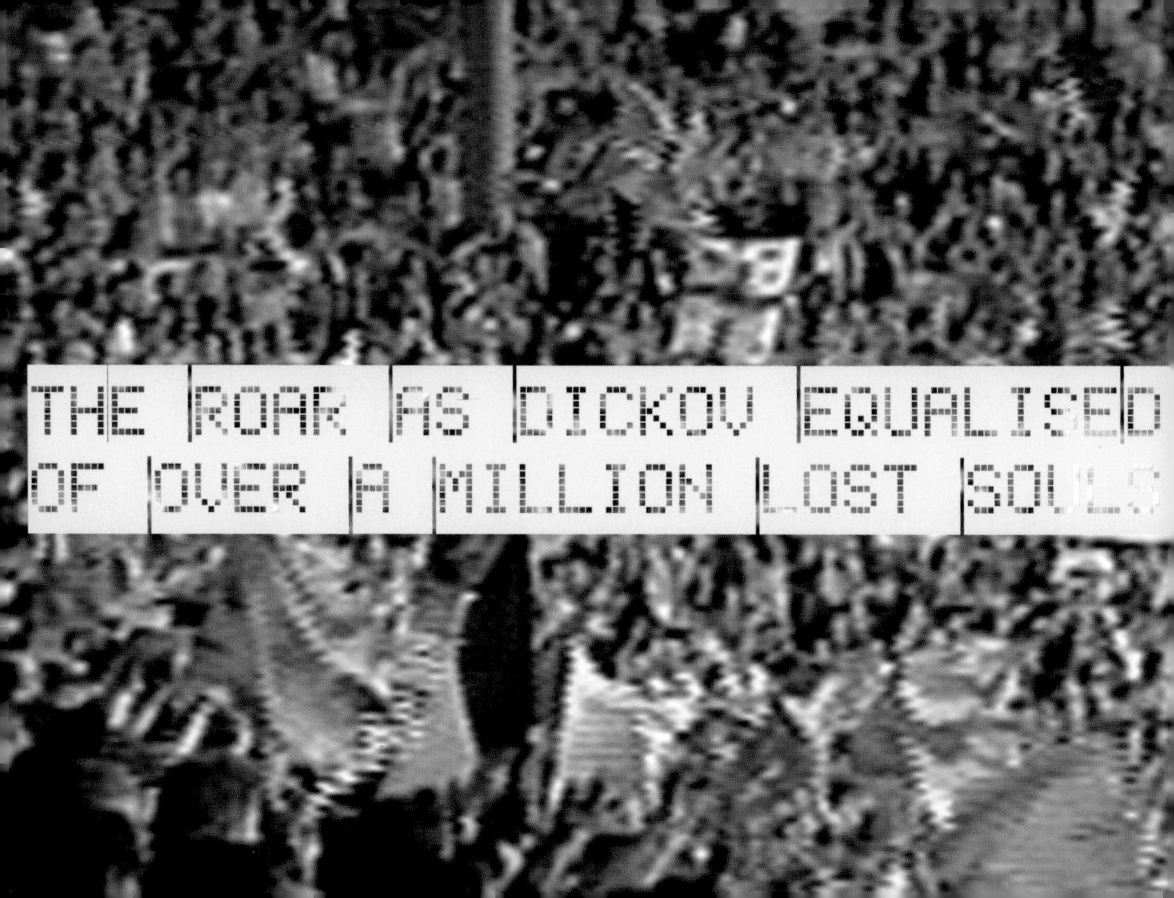

THE ROAR AS DICKOV EQUALISED
OF OVER A MILLION LOST SOULS

IS THE PERSONIFICATION
SCREAMING AS ONE.

DAVID KILROY

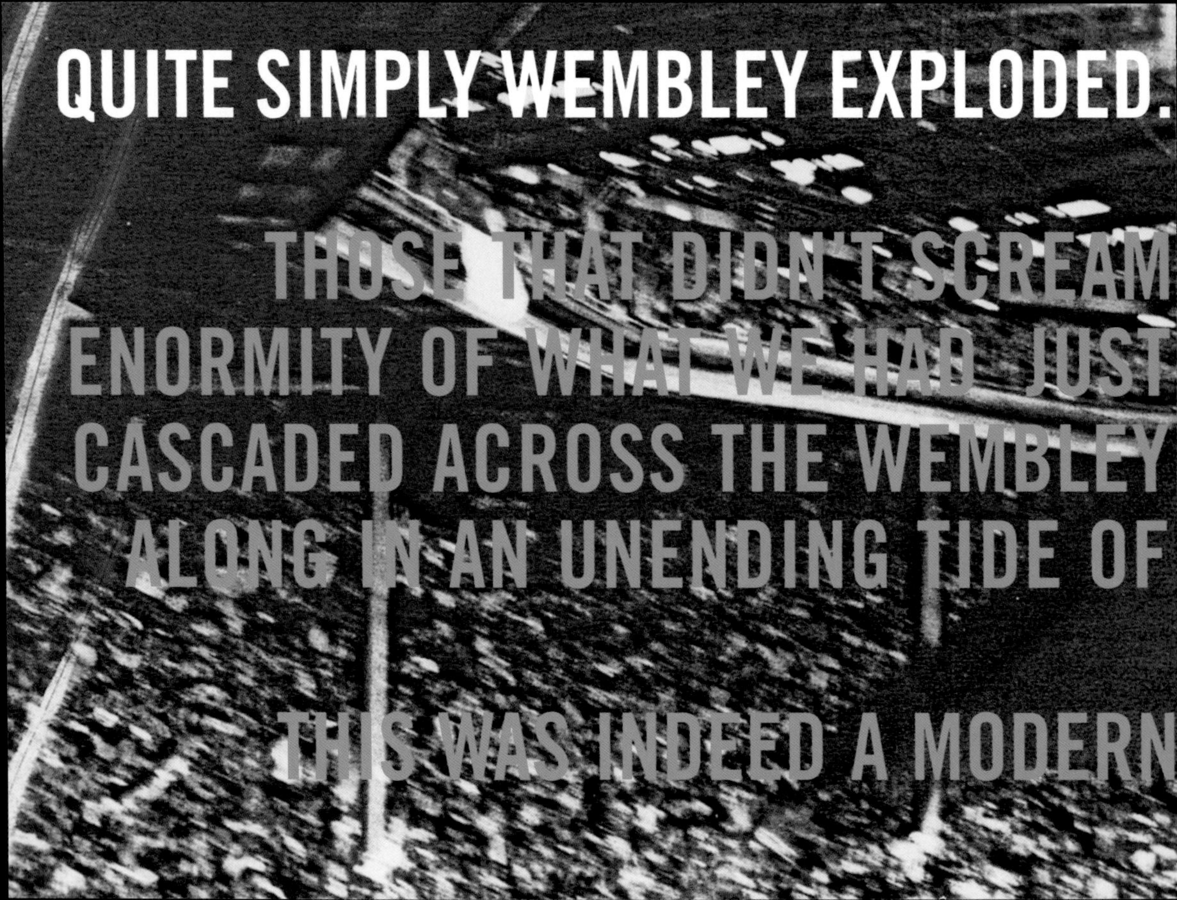

QUITE SIMPLY WEMBLEY EXPLODED.

THOSE THAT DIDN'T SCREAM
ENORMITY OF WHAT WE HAD JUST
CASCADED ACROSS THE WEMBLEY
ALONG IN AN UNENDING TIDE OF

THIS WAS INDEED A MODERN

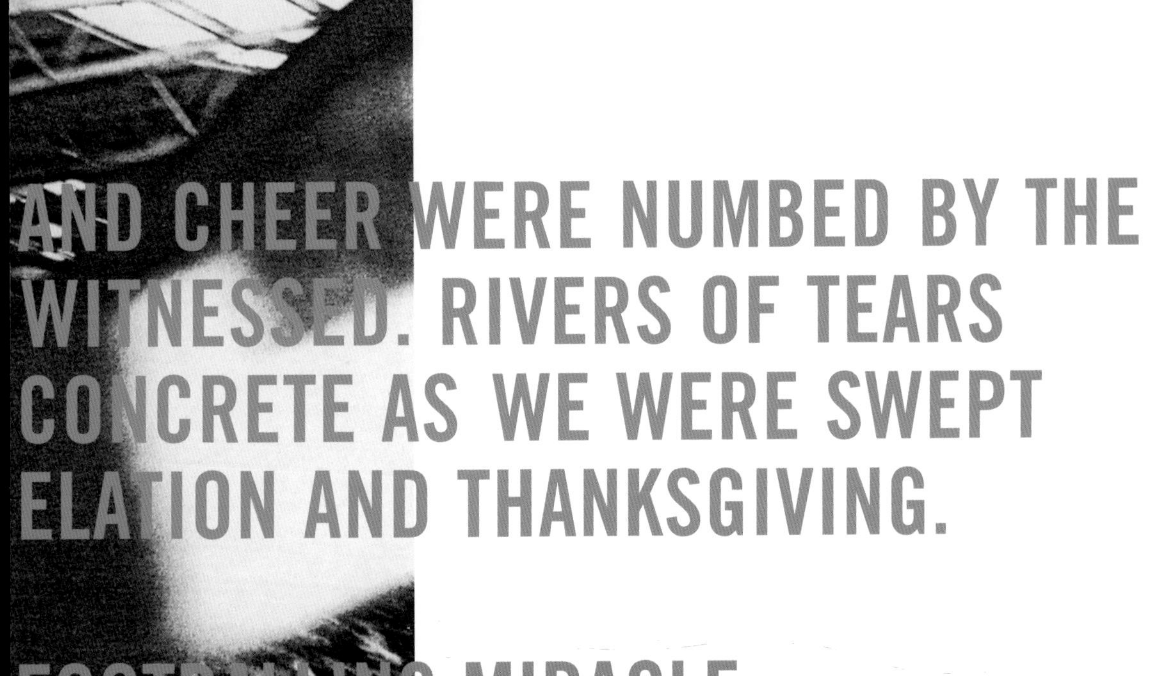

AND CHEER WERE NUMBED BY THE
WITNESSED. RIVERS OF TEARS
CONCRETE AS WE WERE SWEPT
ELATION AND THANKSGIVING.

FOOTBALLING MIRACLE.

TONY BURNS.

0-2. DID YOU STAY OR DID YOU GO?

I was worried about my Dad who is 70. I only made it just outside by the burger vans when we too heard the Wembley roar. I looked at my Dad in tears, he simply said,

"I THINK CITY ARE

CALLING YOU BACK IN".

Berkshire Blue

THAT'S THE FIRST TIME I HAVE EVER LEFT A CITY MATCH EARLY.

WE STARTED THE LONG WALK BACK WITH ALL THE REST...I CAN'T DESCRIBE HOW LOW WE WERE.

THE FIRST ROAR, THE FIRST GOAL, WERE MERELY A CONSOLATION.

THE SECOND, I JUST DIDN'T BELIEVE IT. SO I PHONED MY

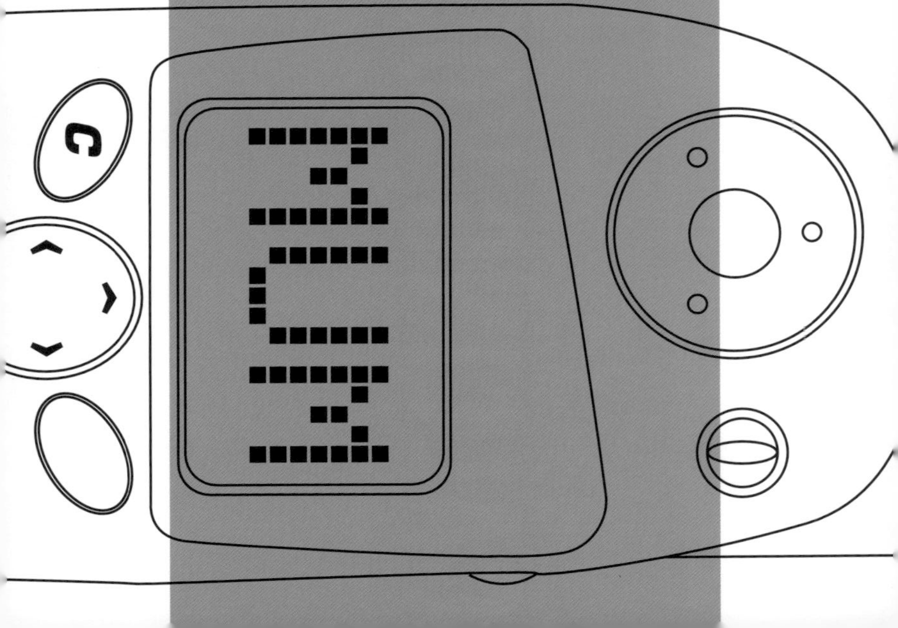

MUM

“MUM, WHAT’S THE SCORE”

“BUT YOU’RE AT WEMBLEY”

“JUST TELL ME THE SCORE”

“2-2, OF COURSE...”

“YEEEEEEESSSSSSSSSS!!!!!!”

I RAN BACK UP WEMBLEY WAY
WAVING MY PHONE HIGH IN
THE AIR, SCREAMING ALOUD,
“IT’S TRUE, IT’S TRUE!”.

BLUE ORACLE.

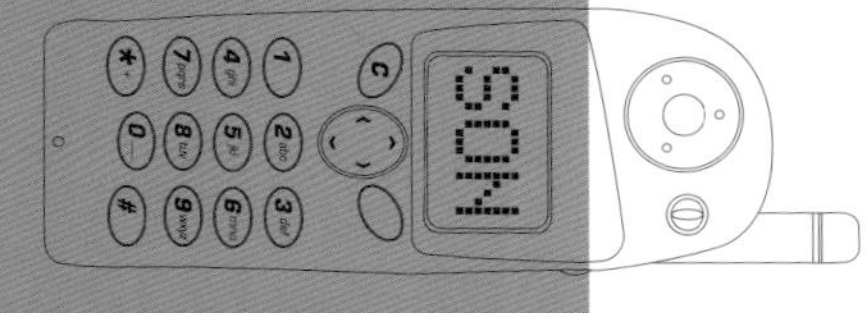

GAN ATHLETIC / MANC

K ROW SEA

03 8 1

RNSTILE F

£32.00

100 1035 150599 16

TWO NIL DOWN, I LEFT.
ON THE WAY OUT I PASSED
THE SCALPER WHO'D SOLD
ME MY TICKET FOR £100
EARLIER IN THE DAY.
HE APOLOGISED AND GAVE
ME FORTY QUID BACK.

CAL LOFTUS.

:14A

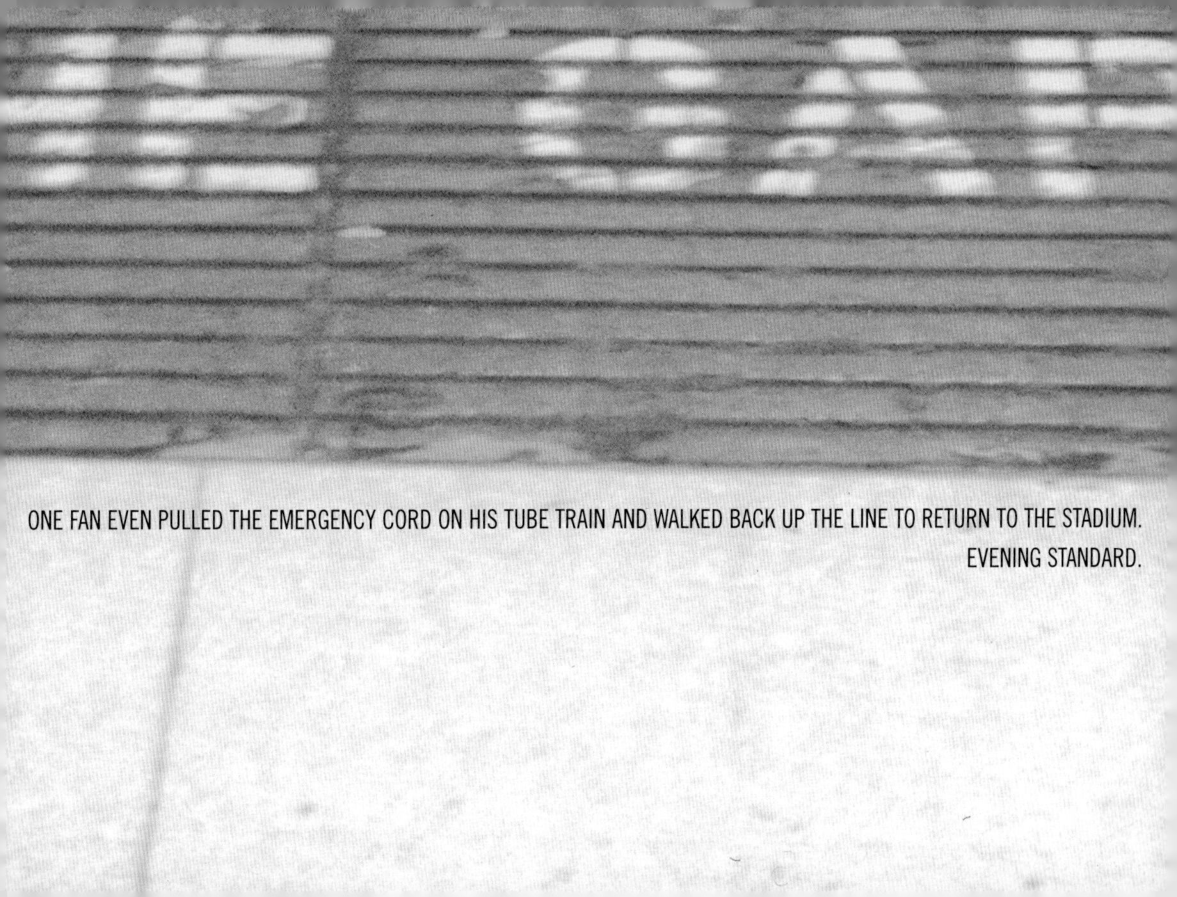

ONE FAN EVEN PULLED THE EMERGENCY CORD ON HIS TUBE TRAIN AND WALKED BACK UP THE LINE TO RETURN TO THE STADIUM.

EVENING STANDARD.

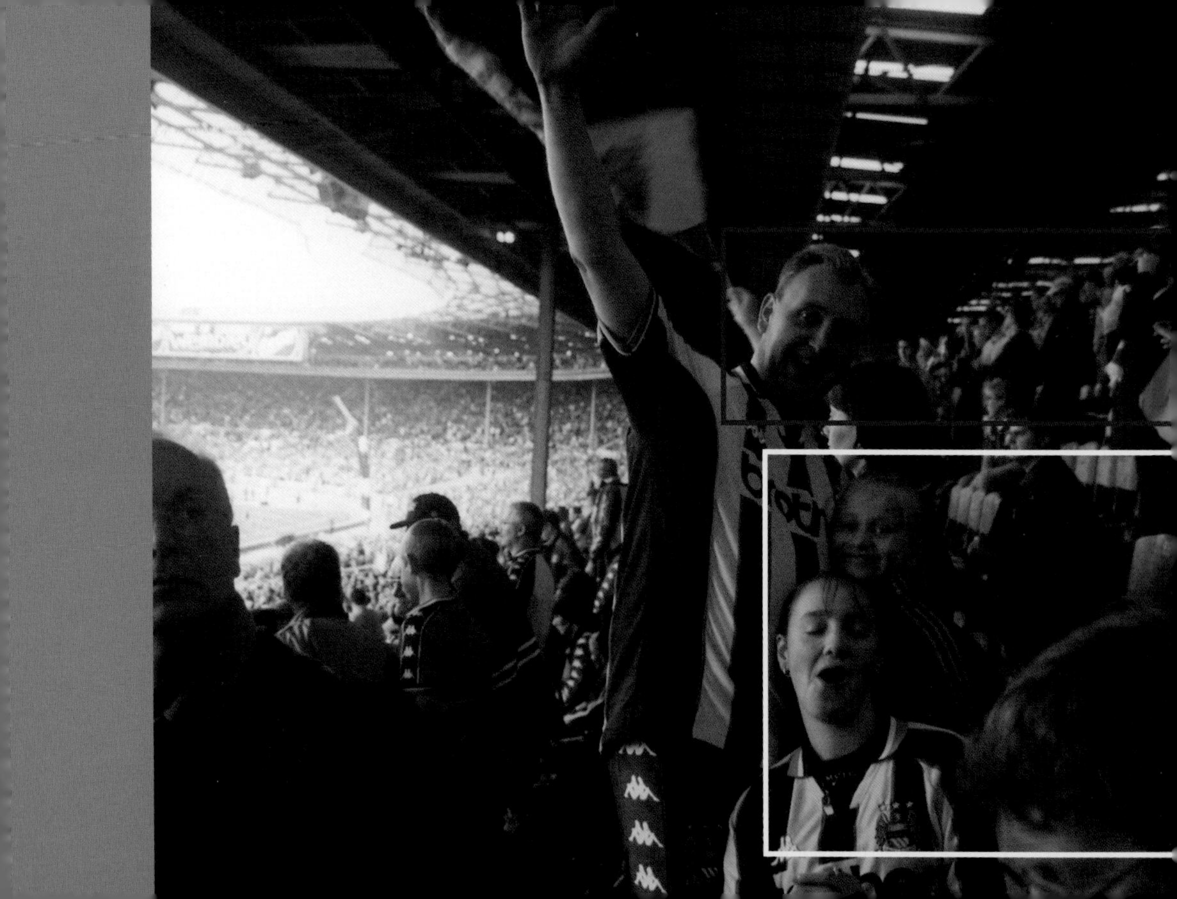

2:

THEY HAVE BEEN AS LOW, AND AS HIGH, IN 10 MINUTES AS US OLD BEGGARS HAVE BEEN IN 20, 30 OR 40 YEARS.

ChinnorBLU

1:

THE YOUNG ONES WHO WERE ALL SO GUTTED AT 0-2 WILL NEVER SUPPORT ANYONE ELSE NOW, THAT'S FOR SURE.

I had to write and tell you who was responsible for it all. Not as you may have thought the team, the management or the chairman, but my own dear mother. You see she died just before the York game in December, having been told she had cancer only a few months before. A life long Blue, she was the one responsible for turning me into one. Now you may be feeling a bit uneasy, what has this to do with City winning one of the best games EVER to grace Wembley? Well hang onto your hat and I'll tell you. Not long after her death I went with my wonderful girlfriend, Helen (known on Blue View as Murtaz or Blue Rinse), to a very wet and cold Wrexham. Now my good old ma' said that the only thing wrong with City was that they needed a kick up the backside and if she ever got the chance she would provide it. She never got that chance when she was alive, but I KNOW she did when she died. Think back to the way we played in that game, we looked like a different team. Remember the stunning saves that Weaver made that day? There was one where he seemed to hang in the air for an age, well that was my mum holding him up there! Game after game the team came out looking like they had had a kick up the backside, time and time again they dug deep, made saves they would never have made before, scored goals that would never have gone in before. My mum was everywhere, on the goal line, on the far post, in the penalty area knocking it down for Goater.

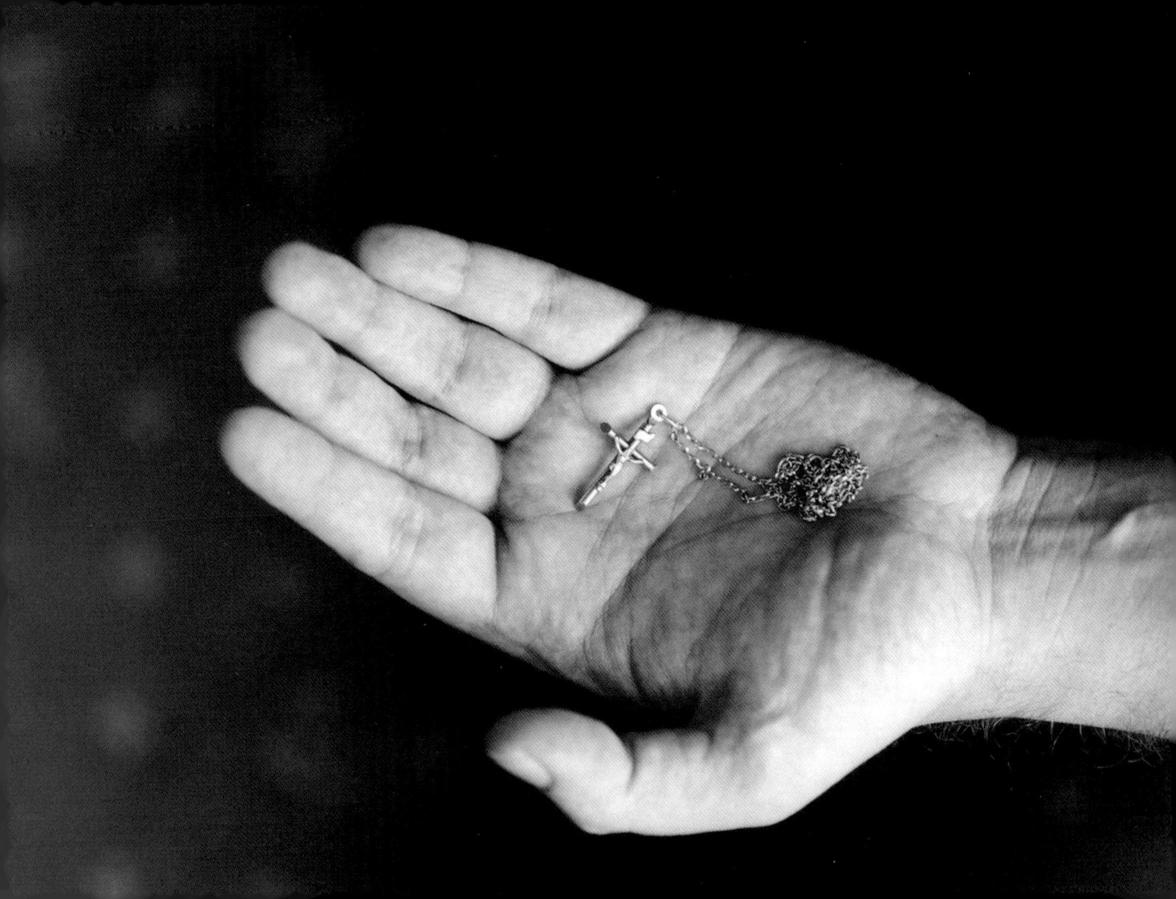

Then came Wembley. For all those who were not there, for all those who left early, don't feel bad. I was there, I did not leave, but I did not see ONE of our goals. When we were two - nil down, I buried my head into my hands, held my crucifix and prayed. I prayed to God, I prayed to my Mother, I prayed so hard that my hands bore the imprint of my cross. I did not see any of the goals until later that night. My mum came through again! She MUST have sneaked on the pitch and turned off the ref's watch, (that's where the 5 minutes came from). So as you see, this season's turn around was all down to a 69 year-old Blue. The letters from people telling how they had gone to the game with their father mother/brother/sister all touched me, because I was there with the two people I love more than anyone, my girlfriend and my mum. What more can a Blue boy want!

Tony Hulme. North Stand Row13 Section N Seat 10

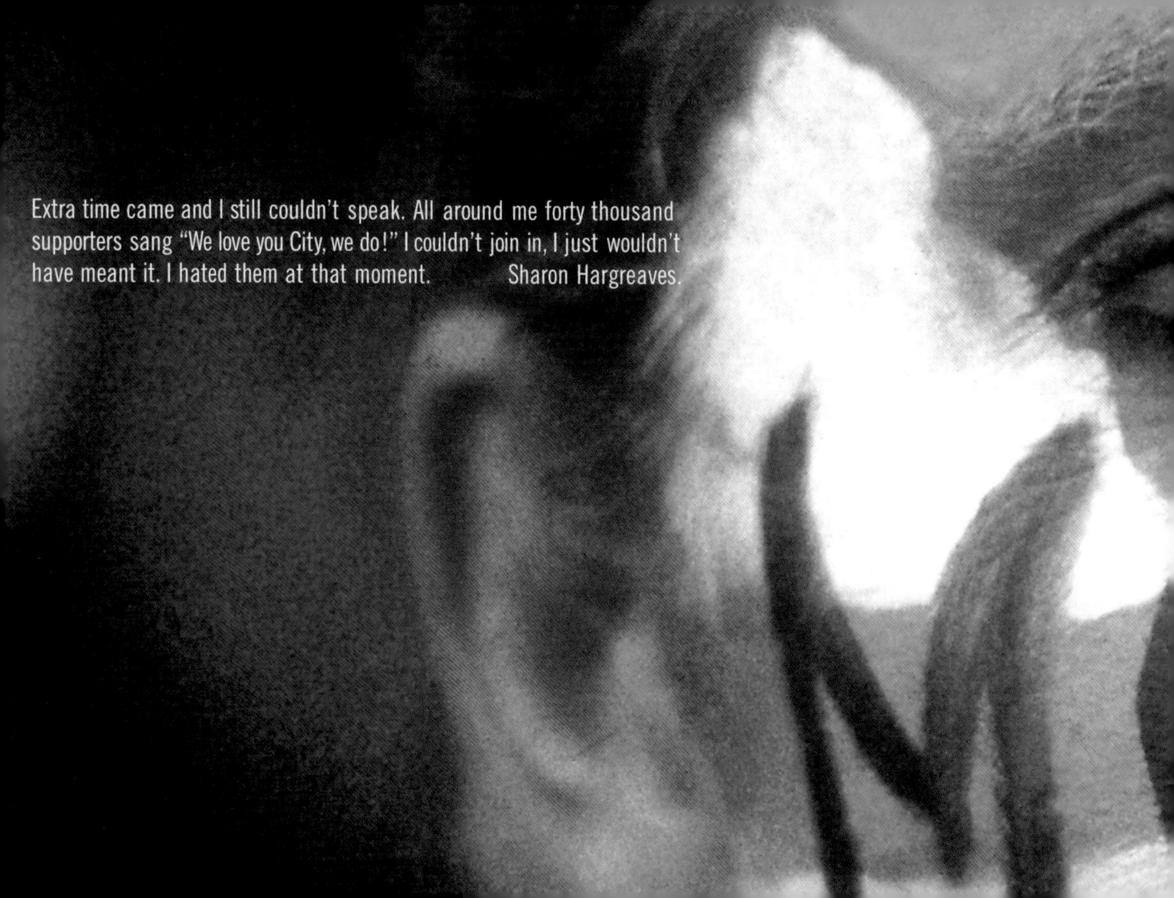

Extra time came and I still couldn't speak. All around me forty thousand supporters sang "We love you City, we do!" I couldn't join in, I just wouldn't have meant it. I hated them at that moment. Sharon Hargreaves.

MC

Horlock /

Dickov X

Cooke /

Edghill /

Goater

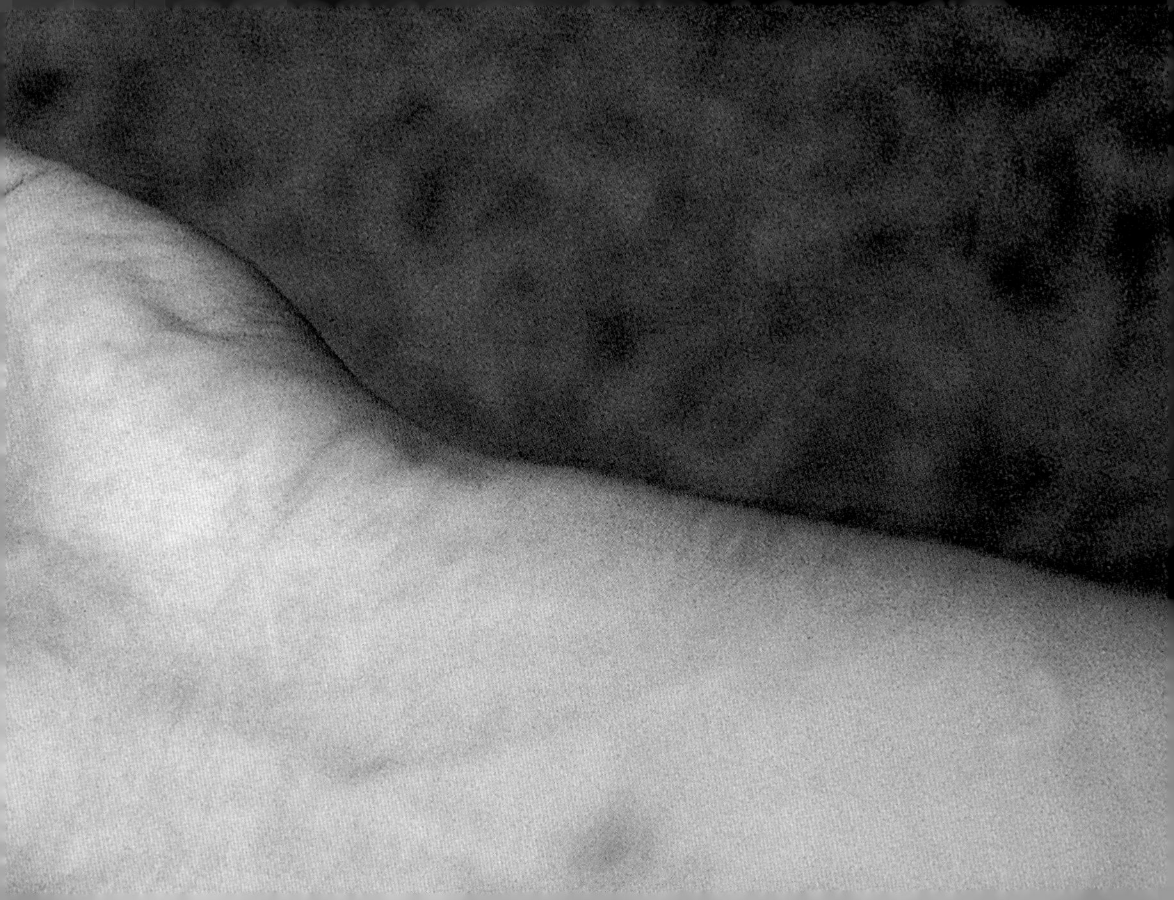

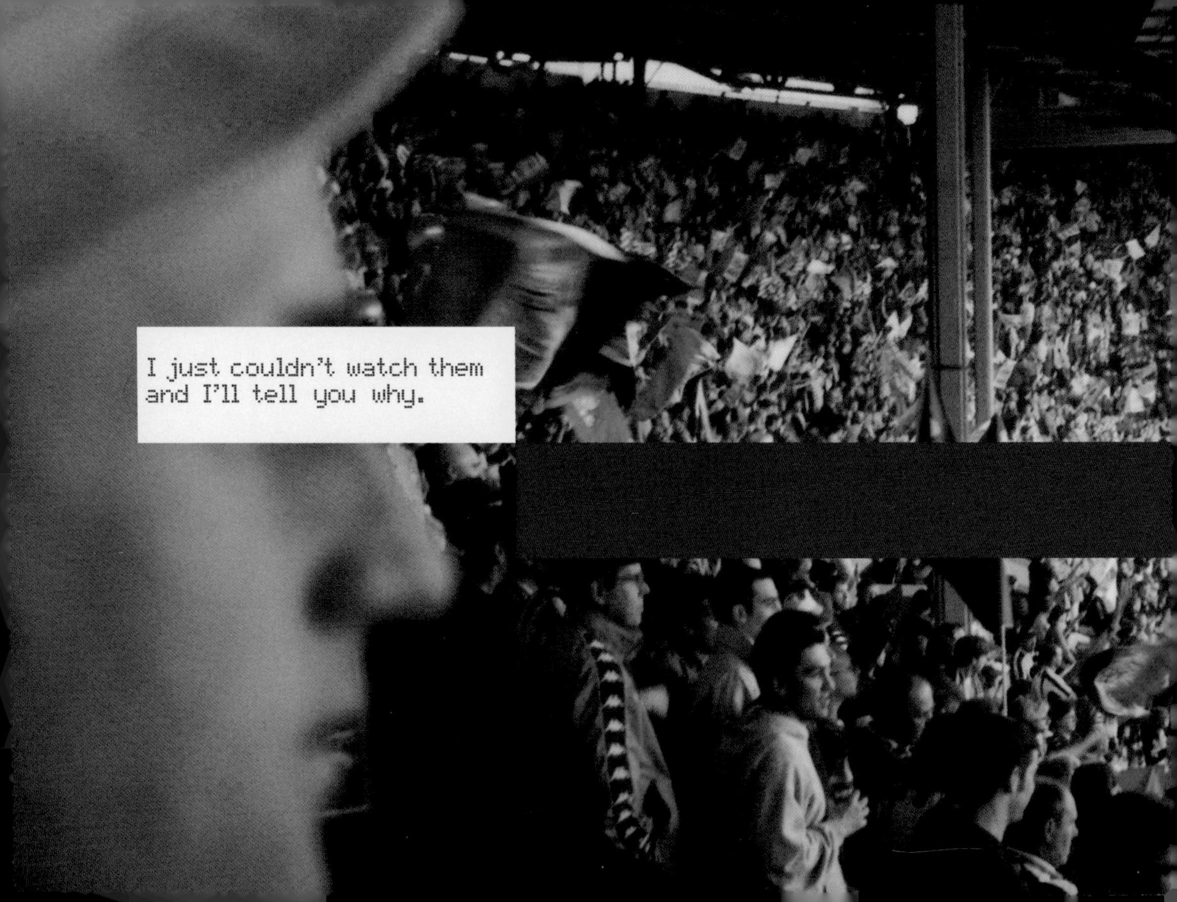
I just couldn't watch them and I'll tell you why.

If me watching City was helping them win they'd have done that in normal or extra time. So I thought, "Okay, I won't watch and see what that does".

Florida Blue

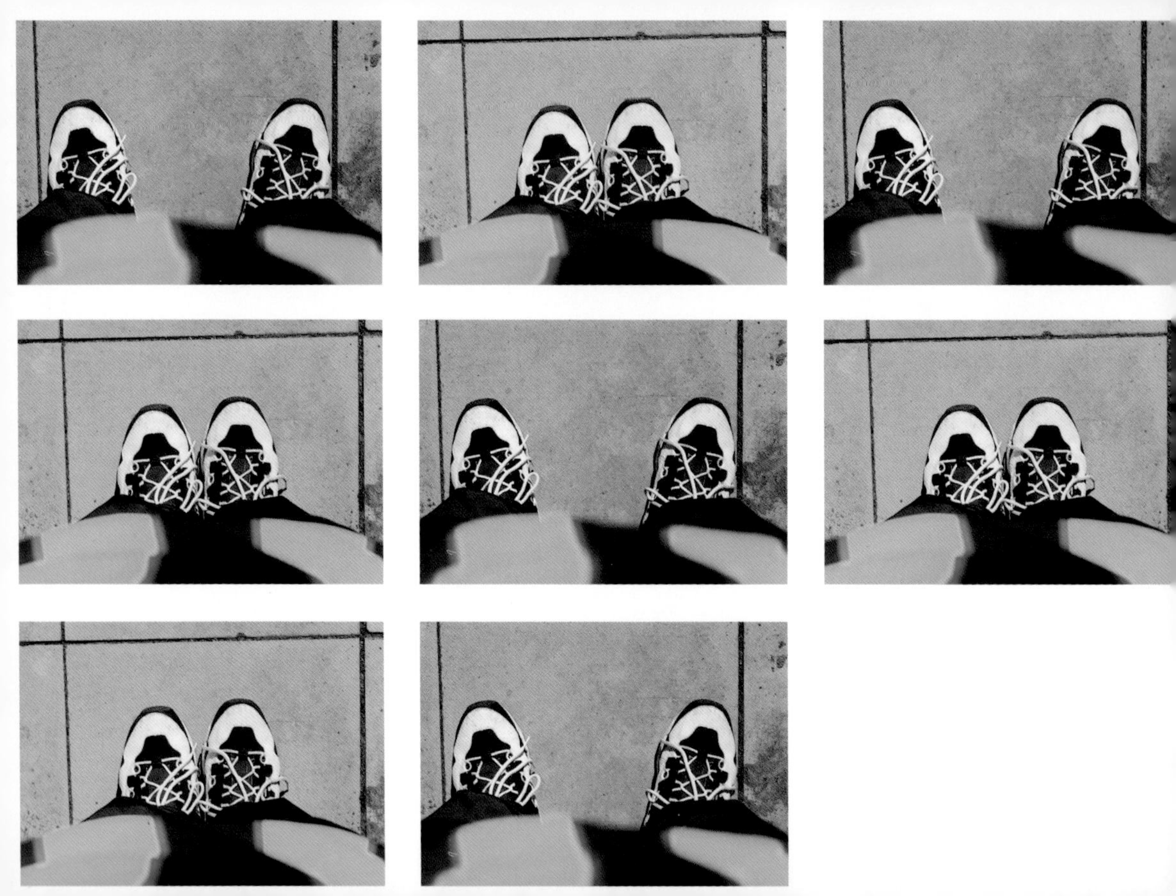

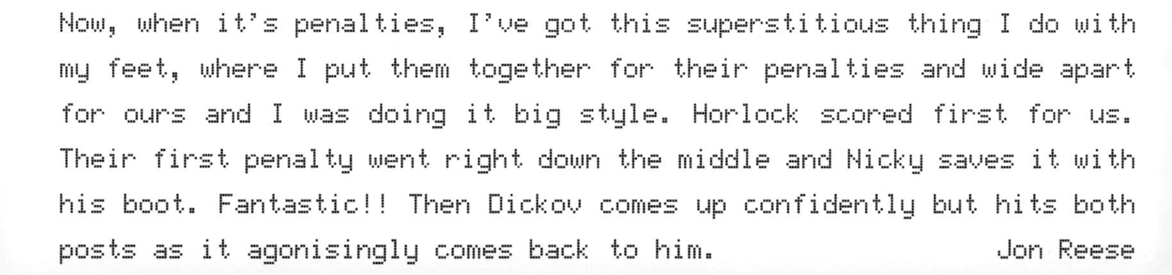

Now, when it's penalties, I've got this superstitious thing I do with my feet, where I put them together for their penalties and wide apart for ours and I was doing it big style. Horlock scored first for us. Their first penalty went right down the middle and Nicky saves it with his boot. Fantastic!! Then Dickov comes up confidently but hits both posts as it agonisingly comes back to him.

Jon Reese

YELLOW COPY TO OPPONENTS
GREEN COPY TO REFEREE
PINK COPY FOR MEDIA USE

TEAM SHEET

Date 30-5-99

MANCHESTER CITY

versus

GILLINGHAM

Referee:- MR. M. HALSEY

Shirt No.	
1	Goalkeeper NICK WEAVER
2	LEE CROOKS
3	RICHARD EDGHILL
4	GERARD WIEKENS
5	ANDY (CAPT) MORRISON
6	KEVIN HORLOCK
7	MICHAEL BROWN
8	JEFF WHITLEY
9	PAUL DICKOV
10	SEAN GOATER
11	TERRY COOKE

Shirt No.	Nominated Substitutes	Replaced	Time
12	GARETH TAYLOR		
13	TONY VAUGHAN		
14	IAN BISHOP		

We are playing in the following colours:

Shirts BLUE - YELLOW STRIPES

Shorts BLUE

Stockings YELLOW

Goalkeeper's Shirt ORANGE

Signed

Official responsible for the Team.

MANCHESTER CITY F.C.

"THEIR SECOND MAN STEPS UP AND THE BLUES' FANS DECIDE THAT THEY WILL BE THE ONES TO SEE CITY THROUGH TO DIVISION ONE. THERE'S EVEN MORE NOISE THAN THE FIRST TIME. MY EARS HURT. THE POOR GILLINGHAM PLAYER HITS IT TOWARDS THE TOP CORNER OF THE NET BUT THE CROWD SUCK IT WIDE." PETER LLEWELLYN

Referee:- MR. M. HALSEY

Shirt No.		Name (printed)	Name (handwritten)
1	Goalkeeper	[illegible] DARVILL	N[illegible] WEAVER
2		[illegible]MON QUAYLE	LEE CROOKS
3		[illegible]HARON HARGREAVES	[illegible]HILL
4		GRAHAM STUART COLE	GE[illegible] WIEKENS
5		[illegible] HULME	ANDY (CAPT) MORRISON
6		DAVID FLATLEY	KEVIN HORLOCK
7		DOUG BELL	BROWN
8		GORDON STUART COLE	JEFF WHITLEY
9		[illegible]CE JOHNSTONE	[illegible] DICKOV
10		DARREN SEDDON	SEAN GOATER
11		[illegible] LAWRENCE	TERRY COOKE

Shirt No.	Nominated Substitutes (printed)	Nominated Substitutes (handwritten)	Replaced	Time
12	STEVE C[illegible]	[illegible]R		
13	ELAINE CLEGG	TONY VAUGHAN		
14	JAGDEER GILL	[illegible]P		

We are playing in the following colours:

Shirts BLUE - YELLOW STRIPES

[illegible]

“THE GILLS FANS TRY TO MAKE OFF-PUTTING SOUNDS BUT THEY’RE AT THE WRONG END.

I HAVE BEEN MORE SCARED IN A MINUTE’S SILENCE.”

PETER LLEWELLYN

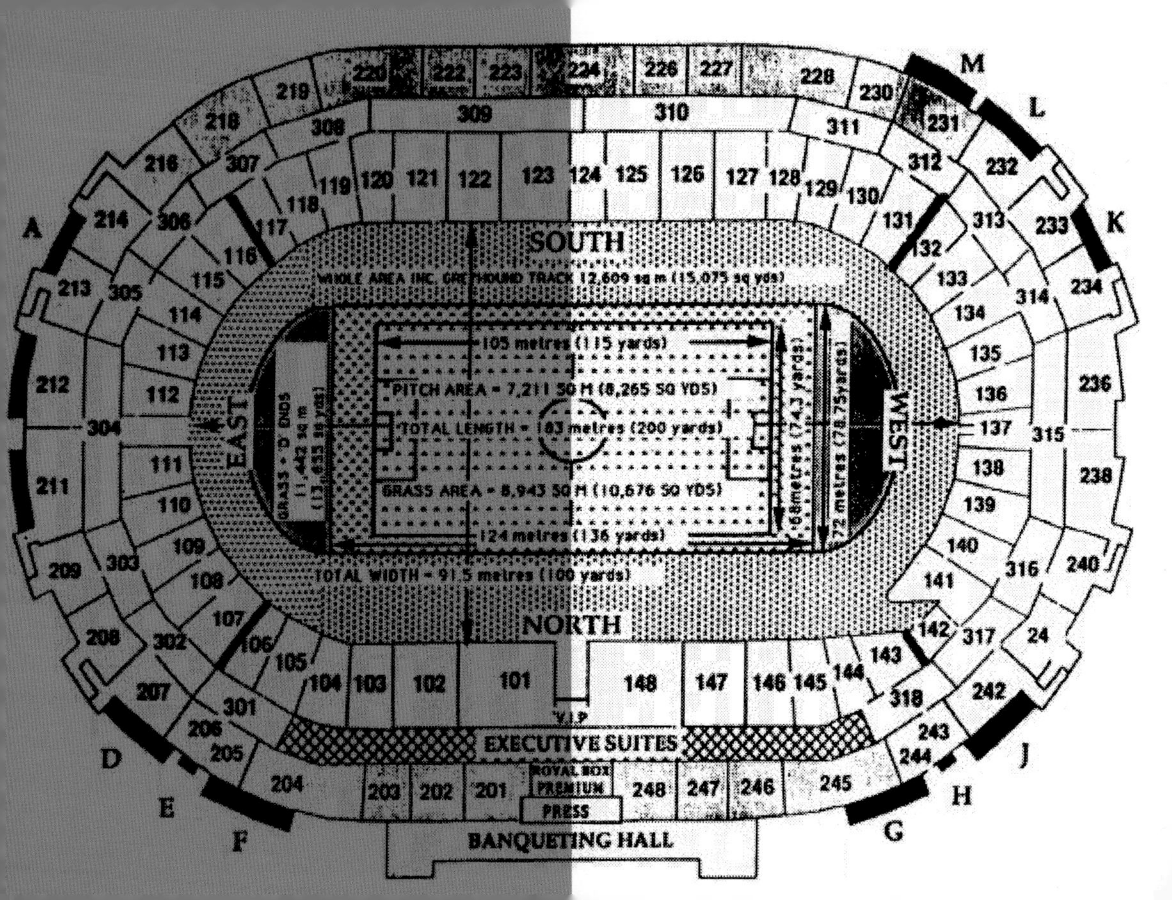
SOUTH
NORTH
EAST
WEST
WHOLE AREA INC. GREYHOUND TRACK 12,609 sq m (15,075 sq yds)
105 metres (115 yards)
PITCH AREA = 7,211 SQ M (8,265 SQ YDS)
TOTAL LENGTH = 183 metres (200 yards)
GRASS AREA = 8,943 SQ M (10,676 SQ YDS)
124 metres (136 yards)
TOTAL WIDTH = 91.5 metres (100 yards)
68metres (74.3 yards)
72 metres (78.75yards)
EXECUTIVE SUITES
V.I.P
ROYAL BOX
PREMIUM
PRESS
BANQUETING HALL
A
D
E
F
G
H
J
K
L
M

At 0-2 down I was feeling frustrated at the thought of spending another season in that awful division. I was also very frustrated and, I have to admit, shouting at people who kept coming up and down the tunnel next to us. For some reason there was a constant procession of people walking backwards and forwards in front of us and it was difficult to concentrate on what was happening on the pitch. Asa Hartford

When Gillingham scored the second goal we were all numb. We discussed this after the game, we all remember looking at each other and without saying a word we all had the same thought, "We've blown it and we'll have to spend another season in the 2nd Division". I think the thought of that spurred us on! When 'Dicky' missed his penalty my thoughts were "I had to score", that was all I was concentrating on. My emotions were another aspect - they were racing, I had hot sweats, started to panic and wondered if my legs would carry me, and to add to it I thought I was deaf from the noise.

Richard Edghill

Kool
Mitre
YES
NO

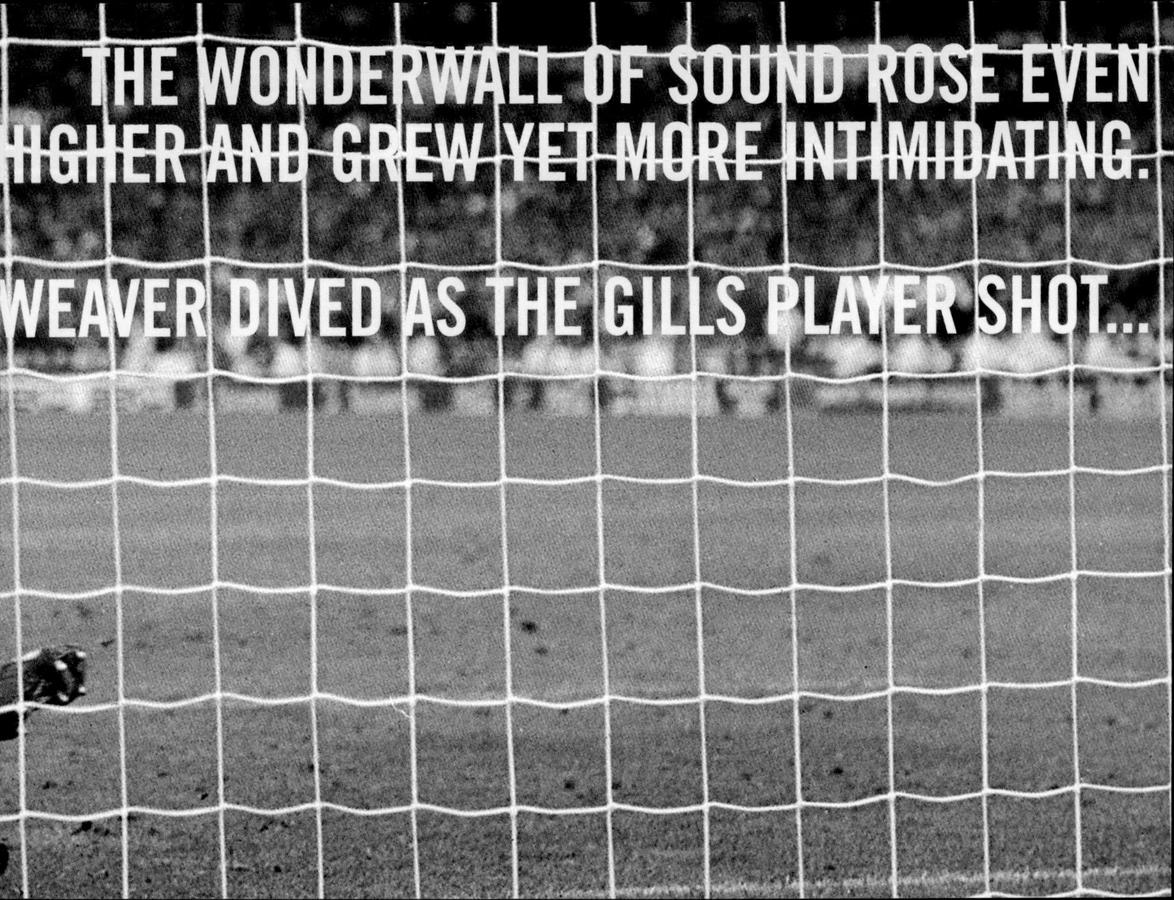
THE WONDERWALL OF SOUND ROSE EVEN
HIGHER AND GREW YET MORE INTIMIDATING.
WEAVER DIVED AS THE GILLS PLAYER SHOT...

YES!

I could feel the tears beginning to well up. Edgy, who I must admit is not my favourite player and never will be, capped a truly great performance by scoring. Then came the deciding moment, if they missed we were up. The emotion was definitely getting to me. Up came Butters, I think it was, and Nicky saved again. I burst into tears. I am not ashamed to say I sobbed my heart out on Maggie's shoulder. I know I vowed after Halifax Town in '79 I would never cry at a football match again, but sod it!

Carol Darvill.

NEVER AGAIN

WHAT CHANCE DID GILLINGHAM REALLY HAVE AGAINST A BRICK WALL OF NOISE; BOOS, WHISTLES AND JEERS, THE LIKE OF WHICH THE TWIN TOWERS HAD NEVER HEARD BEFORE? THEIR ARSES DROPPED OUT AS THEY APPROACHED OUR END FOR THEIR PENALTY KICKS. YOU COULD SEE IT ON THEIR FACES, IN THE WAY THEY WALKED AND MOST IMPORTANTLY IN THEIR PENALTIES. GRAHAM STUART-COLE.

Logged on at 10.30pm South Australian tim
an hour before kick-off. Perused Blue Vie
and sussed out, thanks to other BVers, th
Capital Gold had live and free audio of th
game. Casey was somehow posting still
from the Sky coverage for the fans, player
coming out the tunnel and other pics whic
helped convey the atmosphere to far awa
Blues. Five minutes to kick-off and startin
to tense up now. Logged on to the TalkCit
chat page to be greeted by all the usua
suspects, Herbie, Casey, Oz Blue, Combusti
Cat, Fiji Blue etc etc. Over thirty chatter
online. The first thing I noticed was that bo
Herbie & Casey were about a minute ahea
of the Capital commentary! Very disconcerti
The match is well underway now and stre
levels bordering on the extreme. We all kno
what happens next, all of a sudden it's 2-
to Gillingham. Absolute despair, total an
abject despondency envelops the board
Combustible Cat claims he can't take an
more and logs off! A microcosm of what
happened at Wembley itself!

Herbie has disappeared as well. Looking through spread fingers I begin to type one handed,"... I knew this would F***ing happen, everyone's been far too optimistic...", and then Horlock scores. Typical! Casey then proclaims there are to be five minutes added on. City pour forward and the clock ticks on. 93 minutes gone! It worked before, so looking through spread fingers I begin to type one handed, "... I knew this would F***ing happen etc...", and sure enough we equalise! Cue absolute pandemonium as the message board goes into virtual meltdown. The disbelief, the pure ecstasy was there to behold. Extra Time begins. Chatters are concerned Combustible Cat is missing all the excitement. A quick debate ensues on the merits of whether to inform him or not of the comeback, in case he's the bad luck charm. Eventually it's agreed to try to get him back on. I know his phone number but would have to log off to call him. Fiji Blue offers to call him on his mobile. Nobody knows how to get hold of Herbie. Towards penalties we inexorably roll. Through spread fingers I type one handed, " ...I knew this would F***ing happen etc..." alas this time to no avail. Fiji Blue claims it must be the wrong phone number because all he got through to was an irate woman! Said irate woman is Com Cats partner being told to deny the presence of any City supporters in the household for fear of gloating mates. Phone number checked and confirmed so Fiji Blue calls again! It's 2.30am. A grateful but sheepish Com Cat rejoins the chat.

Penalties it is! The strain is unbearable. Casey, the only one of us with the Sky coverage, doesn't want to watch the penalties. We plead and cajole until he agrees to talk us through it. Then, WEAVER SAVES!!!! Cue mayhem. Indescribable feelings of joy and relief. No-one wants to leave. Everyone wants to linger over this rarest of City performances. Herbie reappears. He had a power failure in his village and had to listen to the rest of the game on the car radio. I finally log off at 3.30am. Tape Sky News and watch the goals over and over again, less than an hour after it has happened. Eventually go to bed and lie awake for two hours before getting up for work. Arrive at work clad in Laser-Blue, totally knackered but unable to wipe the smile off my face.

Bob Lawrence

WE HAD DONE THE IMPOSSIBLE.
THE BOYS DID THEIR BEST.
WE, THE FANS DID OUR BEST.
AS A TEAM, WE GOT THE JOB DONE.
BENJAMIN BLOOM.

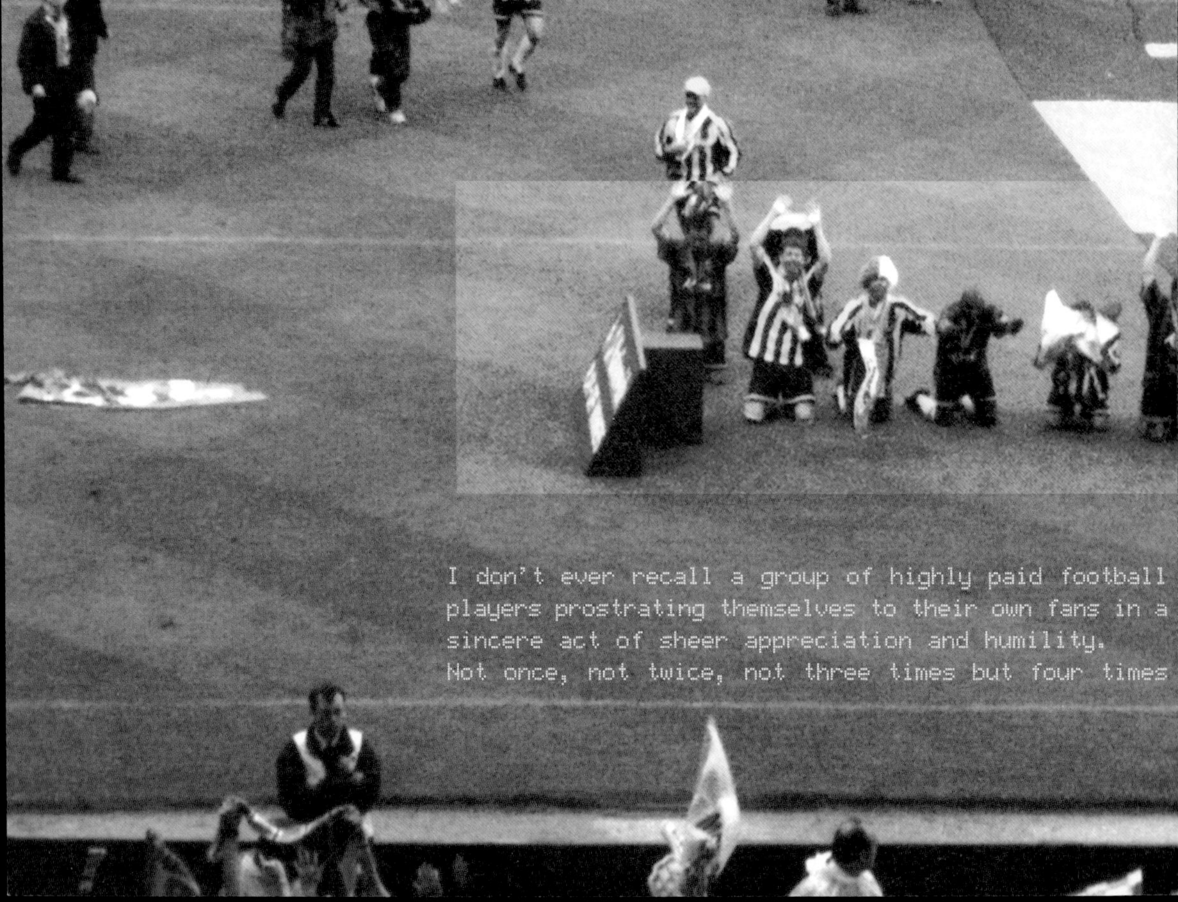

I don't ever recall a group of highly paid football
players prostrating themselves to their own fans in a
sincere act of sheer appreciation and humility.
Not once, not twice, not three times but four times

at each part of the ground that held the Blue Army, our team lay down before us. The unique bond between this crazy club and its fans was once again there for all the world to see, and if truth be known, to envy.

Tony Burns.

16-SEP-1999 19:20 FROM MANAGER

What's your abiding memory of that amazing May afternoon?

walking off the pitch, to 'ours' end looking at a 'sea of ecstasy' singing 'you've got to roll with it'.

When you saw the Blue Army enmasse at Wembley, how did you feel? What contribution do you believe they made to the result?

they never gave up and lifted the team through extra time. the penalties being taken at our end was a massive plus.

SKY SPORTS 2
LIVE

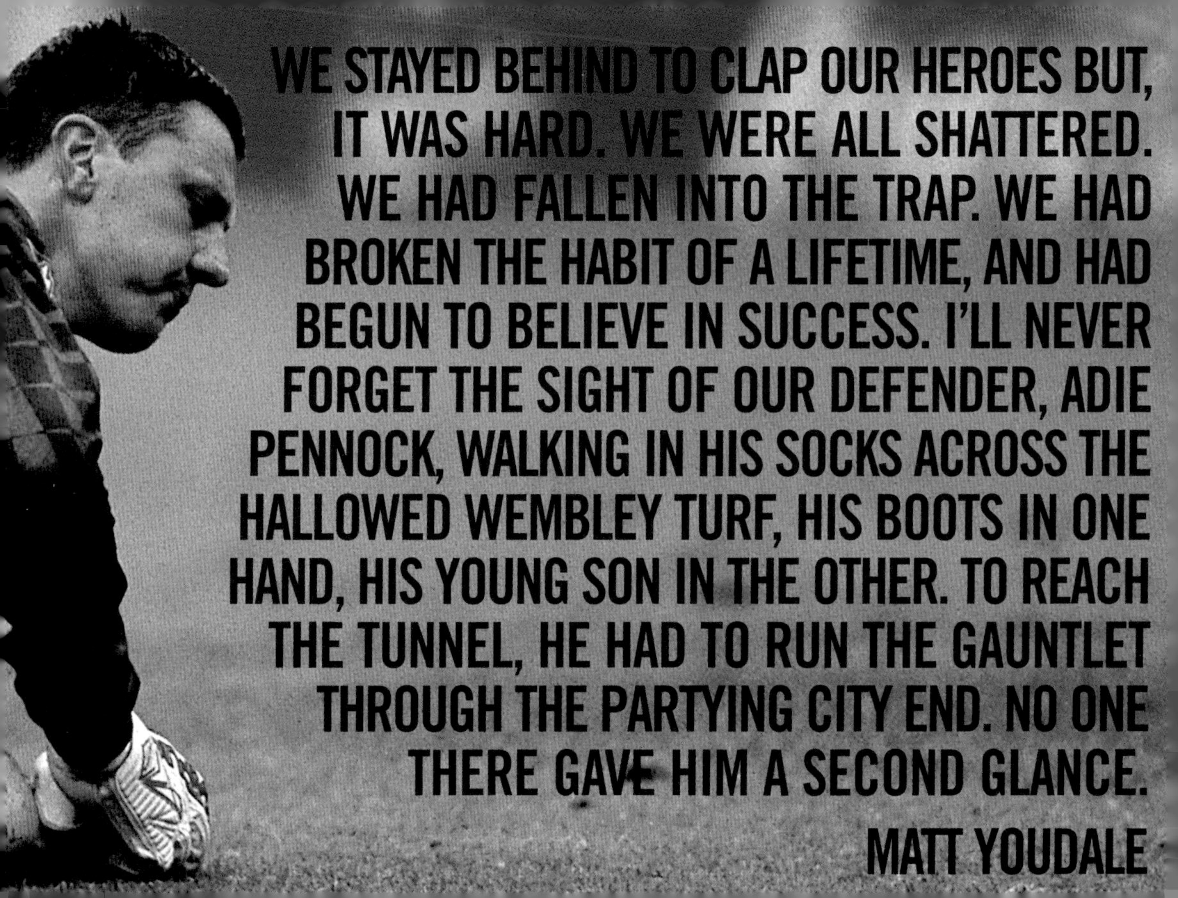
WE STAYED BEHIND TO CLAP OUR HEROES BUT, IT WAS HARD. WE WERE ALL SHATTERED. WE HAD FALLEN INTO THE TRAP. WE HAD BROKEN THE HABIT OF A LIFETIME, AND HAD BEGUN TO BELIEVE IN SUCCESS. I'LL NEVER FORGET THE SIGHT OF OUR DEFENDER, ADIE PENNOCK, WALKING IN HIS SOCKS ACROSS THE HALLOWED WEMBLEY TURF, HIS BOOTS IN ONE HAND, HIS YOUNG SON IN THE OTHER. TO REACH THE TUNNEL, HE HAD TO RUN THE GAUNTLET THROUGH THE PARTYING CITY END. NO ONE THERE GAVE HIM A SECOND GLANCE.
MATT YOUDALE

Dennis Tueart.

What's your abiding memory of that amazing May afternoon?

The club being given its pride back and the sight of the whole of one part of Wembley covered in Blue & White.

What does the battle cry 'City 'til I die' really mean to you?

It gives me a lump in the throat and reminds me of meeting hundreds of City fans at Warwick Services on the M40 coming home from Wembley and seeing them doing the 'Conga' around the Services.

At 2pm on Sunday afternoon I ensconced myself in my bedroom for the T.V. showing of the play-off final. Away strip worn, beer in abundance and the confident thought that City would win easily. Oh, how wrong could I be.

After 80 minutes Gillingham ripped our defence apart and Asaba scored, sh*t, not to worry, there's still time for our gallant lads to come back. Let's face it, we had done it a few times during the latter part of the season. My wife had to field telephone calls from my so-called mates phoning from the pub, gloating bastards. A few minutes later and the whole world fell apart, 2-0 down. Again the wife had phone calls to field, "...do you want to talk to Mick?", "Just tell him to get stuffed." I told her. The shirt came off. I was covered in sweat, nooooooooo this couldn't be happening. I admit I was wondering what another year in the 2nd Division was going to be like. Then a lifeline, Horlock scores a good goal. What's that? Five minutes left, still in with a chance, come on. Shirt once more covering body, I bounce up and down on the bed. Yeeeesss...Dicky you little beauty. Extra time was all City, Gillingham had blown it, you could just tell.

And so it all came down to penalties. Horlock looked confident and dispatched his penalty easily. Up stepped the Gillingham player and I could tell just by his body language that he would miss, he just didn't look up for it. Nicky Weaver you beauty! The screaming in the bedroom reached Boeing 747 proportions. Then Richard Edghill, a great penalty taken with great confidence. But then the crowning moment, Nicky Weaver makes himself look even bigger than he really is by stretching his arms wide and pulls off the greatest of saves.

Oh what joy, I almost came through the bloody ceiling.

Geoff Collins.

THE JOYOUS CRAWL BACK UP THE M1.
FLAGS AND SCARVES FLUTTERING
FROM THE WINDOWS AND THE BANNER
ON THE BRIDGE NEAR LUTON,

“WEAVER DONE IT”.

HEIDI PICKUP

My dad was an avid City nut for more than 40 years, he said he remembers the 1956 Cup Final against the mighty Birmingham. He was at St.James Park when City won the League in 1968 as well as all the other finals over the next 13 years. He was Blue mad. He passed away on March 26th this year, but he always maintained City would win the play-offs,

“... a sure thing” he promised.

Steve Cooper

Oh sweet mysteries of life!

Now it was my turn to be David Pleat as my mind raced back to that day in 1983 as well as Colin's testimonial where we cried tears of both sadness and joy for the privilege of paying homage to a supreme talent. Then remembering my stomach churning in the very deepest pit, gnawing, aching at my very soul when we were relegated from the Premiership and THEY had won the title on the very same day. I had travelled all the way from my home in Portsmouth and taken my nine year old son to the last game to see us draw with Liverpool, knowing that the 'Scummers' (our local Pompey term for Southampton) had survived at our expense! I'll never forget my poor boy's tears and the ridicule he underwent when I walked him back to my brother's house in Longsight, for as we approached the front door we spotted the grotesque, life size picture of a particularly nasty Frenchman holding aloft the Premiership trophy and the banner 'Glory, Glory Man. Utd.'

So you see, we are enjoying our day in the sun, and this is retribution for the cold dark winter recess which has bedridden our once proud and successful club for far too long. I truly believe that this victory will act as the catalyst to enable the Phoenix to rise and once again soar with the Eagles. I just love, love, love our club with all my heart.

Hugh Doyle

PAST
THE FOOTBALL LEAGUE

M.C.F.C.
Superbia In Proelio

PAST PRES

That Sunday afternoon in May saw an epiphany, a rebirth of a sleeping giant, the sorry slide is over and City are on the way back. The days at Portsmouth in the rain, drafty and cramped Loftus Road and the misery of Stockport are not entirely behind us, but we have looked over the edge of the abyss and have saved ourselves. The loyalty of the fans and perseverance of both the manager and the players have shown us that there is another way for City. I shall remember what yesterday felt like forever, but we are only a few steps along what must be a long, difficult march. Tomorrow a sense of perspective can return, but we can now dream that one day a City captain will lift a proper trophy. That dream can now live on and perhaps those who have mocked us will understand a little better the proud boast, "City 'til I die!"

Simon Quayle.

NTFUTURE

M.C.F.C.
brother

Two-nil down, I just sat there and cried. With only minutes left they had managed to mess up what should have been the greatest day of my Blue life.

This was to be my last match at Maine Road before my family up-rooted and left for a new life in Australia. It had all begun so well. My dad had secretly arranged an audience for me with my hero, Joe Corrigan. Joe in turn organised a team photo, a tour of the ground and finally, the trophy room. It was to be a day of priceless memories.

Sitting in the North Stand with only a few minutes to go, Spurs were leading two-nil. My last ever visit to Maine Road was rapidly heading towards disaster. How could it possibly end this way? I remember my Dad gently asking whether I wanted to leave. I could only blurt out a blubbering "No!".

My faith was rewarded as City pulled back two last gasp goals to level the scores at full-time. As 'Big Joe' applauded our section of the crowd at the end, I swear to this very day that he winked at me!

Over sixteen years later, on a grey May afternoon at Wembley, history repeated itself.

But I guess that shouldn't be a surprise. Supporting Manchester City has always been a tempestuous affair. A life-long commitment that makes agonisingly high demands of all of us. Yet occasionally, just occasionally, it rewards us with a glimpse of sheer heaven.

Ultimately, Wembley 1999 was just another day at the office for Manchester City.

David Chidlow

umbro

acknowledgments

For Mum, Dad and Spencer William Porter.

Endless thanks, hugs and love to the following for acts above and beyond the call of duty, over the last season: Angela, my family, Simon, Graham, Gordon, Nigel, Becky, Paul, Manita, John, Emma, Matho, Val and Mike.

Thank you to Julian Baskcomb and Julia Byrne at Polar for their continuous support and guidance throughout this project.

Many thanks to Julian Germain for his wonderful portraits and for investing such time and effort on this project.

Large flashing thanks to Stephen Widdows for his still-life shots of City ephemera. stephenwiddows@insomnious.com.

'Racey's Rocket' type thanks to Barrie Mitchell for capturing Dickov's goal in true Melchester Rovers' style!

Manc-thanks to Tony, Helen, Doug, Gary James, Dave Wallace and the writers at 'King of the Kippax', Noel Bayley and his squad at 'Bert Trautmann's Helmet', Sara Billington, David Bernstein and all at Manchester City Football Club.

Thanks to Vic Wakeling and Suzanne Boocock at Sky Sports and Martin Corrie at Wembley National Stadium for their assistance.

Thanks to the good folks at D'Arcy: Colin, Chris, Ed, Leah, Bernie, Matt, Nick, Sarah, David, Natalie, Ben, Ollie, and Don.

Thanks Andy Altman, Patrick Burgoyne, Ben Casey and Beverly Parker for your invaluable advice as to getting this project off the ground.

Finally a big thankyou to all the Blues who contributed to helping capture both that amazing day and what it means to be C'TID!

Published in Great Britain 1999 by Polar Print Group Ltd, 2 Uxbridge Road, Leicester LE4 7ST, England

ISBN 1 899538 71 2

Printed by Polar Print Group Ltd, 2 Uxbridge Road, Leicester LE4 7ST Telephone (0116) 261 0800

Photographs courtesy of: SkySports, Empics, Professional Sport U.K. and Manchester Evening News. Most remaining photographs are from the private collection of the author or from those of other supporters. Stadium plan & stub courtesy of Wembley National Stadium Ltd.

Sincere thanks to Doug Bell for entrusting me with his family snapshots. 1998/99 ticket stub collection courtesy of Graham Stuart-Cole.

e-mail: Wembley1999@hotmail.com

AT 6AM ON MO[illegible]
MORNING OUR 3 YE[illegible]
OLD SON WAS O[illegible]
MY CHEST SINGING

AIRSONY ON
MICKY WEAVER
ON MICKY WEAVER!

HE'S A BIT YOUNG FOR
MAINE RD. NOW, BUT IN
A FEW YEARS... THIS IS
JUST THE START!

NIGEL